BELT AND ROAD

Business with China

Series Editor: Kerry Brown

The titles in this series explore the complex relationship between Chinese society and China's global economic role. Exploring a wide range of issues, the series challenges the view of a country enclosed in on itself and shows how the decisions made by Chinese consumers, the economic and political choices made by its government and the fiscal policies followed by its bankers are impacting on the rest of the world.

Published

Belt and Road: The First Decade
Igor Rogelja and Konstantinos Tsimonis

China's Hong Kong: The Politics of a Global City
Tim Summers

The Future of UK–China Relations: The Search for a New Model
Kerry Brown

BELT AND ROAD

The First Decade

Igor Rogelja and Konstantinos Tsimonis

agenda
publishing

To Silas, Daphne & Lydia

First published in 2023 by Agenda Publishing

Agenda Publishing Limited
The Core
Bath Lane
Newcastle Helix
Newcastle upon Tyne
NE4 5TF
www.agendapub.com

ISBN 978-1-78821-253-3 (hardcover)
ISBN 978-1-78821-254-0 (paperback)

British Library Cataloguing-in-Publication Data
A catalogue record for this book is available from the British Library

Typeset by Newgen Publishing UK
Printed and bound in the UK by 4edge Limited

Contents

Acknowledgements

We wrote this book during a time of heightened polarization of the public debate on China in Europe. The free and stimulating intellectual environments of the European and International Social and Political Studies Department at University College London and of the Lau China Institute at King's College London, where we are respectively based, allowed us to reflect on the Belt and Road and shielded us from the pressure of having to pick a side as "pro-" or "anti-" China advocates. Scholarly work is relevant to policymakers but we must resist the temptation of adjusting our approach to sound more relevant or in tune with the geopolitical zeitgeist. After extensive politicking in the second half of the last decade, we are glad to witness more balanced and cool-headed narratives on China emerging again. We hope that this book contributes to such an informed debate on the Belt and Road and its many challenges and opportunities.

The first round of thanks begins with Professor Kerry Brown, who pitched the idea of this book to us a few years ago. Throughout the writing process, he has provided comments and feedback that have helped us revisit and sharpen our arguments. We are grateful for his support, encouragement and academic example. Our decision to work on global China was inspired by the scholarship of Professor Julia Strauss, our former PhD supervisor, who was one of the early researchers of Chinese investments in Latin America and Africa. We are also very grateful for the critical comments and valuable suggestions by the anonymous peer reviewers. Their constructive feedback and criticism helped us substantially improve the proposal and the final manuscript.

This book was in many ways formed through collaborations and conversations we had with colleagues and peers. It is impossible to thank everyone but we would like to mention Ben Barratt, Martina Bofulin, Megan Bowman, Anastasia Frantzeskaki, Zeng Jinghan, Jan Knoerich, Evangelos Raftopoulos and Richard Turcsányi for their insights and advice, not to mention their work and scholarly example.

The book benefited greatly from two grants that we received from the King's Together Fund and the BA/Leverhulme Small Research Grants scheme, which have facilitated our own work on the Belt and Road in Europe and the Balkans. We are grateful to the research support team of the School of Global Affairs at King's, especially Lyanne Wylde and James Gagen, for helping us to navigate through the complex processes of applying for and spending those grants.

Alison Howson and the team at Agenda Publishing provided excellent support during all stages of writing and publication. Special thanks go to Anca Crowe, Hai Jiawei and Ivan Butler for their assistance in helping us put together a presentable manuscript. Of course, all remaining errors remain our own.

Last but not least, we recognize that academics can be difficult family members, especially when they are working towards book submission deadlines. Silas, Daphne and Lydia have been a constant source of joy and inspiration. We dedicate this book to them as a small token of our gratitude and affection.

Acronyms and abbreviations

AIIB	Asian Infrastructure Investment Bank
ASEAN	Association of Southeast Asian Nations
BHRRC	Business & Human Rights Resource Centre
BRI	Belt and Road Initiative
CCP	Chinese Communist Party
CDB	China Development Bank
CEEC	Cooperation between China and Central and Eastern European Countries
CHEG	China Harbour Engineering Group
COSCO	China Ocean Shipping Company
CPEC	China–Pakistan Economic Corridor
CRBC	China Road and Bridge Corporation
CSR	corporate social responsibility
EIA	Environmental Impact Assessment
EU	European Union
FDI	foreign direct investment
FIC	Forum for International Cooperation
FOCAC	Forum on China–Africa Cooperation
GDI	Global Development Initiative
GDP	gross domestic product
GWD	Great Western Development
ICBC	Industrial and Commercial Bank of China
IMF	International Monetary Fund
LRT	light rail transit
LSG	leading small group
MDB	multilateral development bank
MFA	Ministry of Foreign Affairs

MOFCOM	Ministry of Commerce of the People's Republic of China
MoU	memorandum of understanding
NATO	North Atlantic Treaty Organization
NDRC	National Development and Reform Commission
NGO	non-governmental organization
OECD	Organisation for Economic Co-operation and Development
OEEC	Organisation for European Economic Cooperation
PCT	Piraeus Container Terminal
PH	Pakatan Harapan
PLA	People's Liberation Army
PPA	Piraeus Port Authority
PRC	People's Republic of China
PSC	private security company
SASAC	State-owned Assets Supervision and Administration Commission
SCO	Shanghai Cooperation Organization
SEZ	special economic zone
SGR	standard-gauge railway
SOE	state-owned enterprise
TEAS	Tebian Electric Apparatus Stock Co. Ltd
TEU	twenty-foot equivalent unit
UN	United Nations
UNODC	United Nations Office on Drugs and Crime
WGI	World Bank's World Governance Indicators
WTO	World Trade Organization

What is this book about?

After years of struggling under austerity imposed by European partners and a chilly shoulder from the United States, Greece has embraced the advances of China, its most ardent and geopolitically ambitious suitor ... While Europe was busy squeezing Greece, the Chinese swooped in with bucket-loads of investments that have begun to pay off, not only economically but also by apparently giving China a political foothold in Greece, and by extension, in Europe.

Horowitz and Alderman (2017)

In Greece, China has used its checkbook to take the port of Piraeus, ... accomplishing what the Persian King Xerxes failed to do with overwhelming force twenty-five hundred years ago. Hillman (2020: 23)

A train of thought that presents China's global economic activities as an attempt at political domination has become commonplace over the last decade. Books, journal articles, policy reports and political speeches from around the world began to warn of China's new-found assertiveness. At the same time, Xi Jinping suddenly seemed eager to loudly proclaim his ambitions and emerge from the sidelines of global politics. Take the examples above, which suggest China used economic power as a way to acquire a political foothold in Greece (where even Xerxes failed, no less). What motives might the authors be suggesting? To what ends will this "political foothold" be used? Will China build a new Sinocentric world order? Will it push out the US and the West, one country at a time? Will it write the last chapter of its long revenge for the century of humiliation? This appealing argument has captured public imagination about the Belt and Road Initiative (BRI, the Initiative, sometimes called "OBOR" due to its Mandarin name *yi dai yi lu* 一带一路, literally "One Belt One Road"). However, there are four main problems with the logic behind this perception that prompted us to write this book at the end of the BRI's first decade.

The first issue is that this narrative is self-perpetuating and addictive. If we start off believing that Chinese activities are part of an imperialist plan to dominate the world, we can easily pile up evidence that this is happening simply by reframing all economic deals, loans, trade agreements and new infrastructure projects as shrewd moves on a global chessboard. This is because the alleged motive – global hegemony – is so vague that it allows us to reframe everything that China does as evidence, even dispatching Covid-19 humanitarian aid. The repetitive framing of the activities of Chinese companies as a potential or actual threat to the present world order ultimately becomes addictive, tempting us to interpret all developments through this lens and to create narratives embellished with stereotypes and alarmist language, often using military terms and expressions. As the opening paragraph for this book attests, "threat speech" can easily make its way into any narrative.

The second problem is that the "global domination" logic fails to appreciate nuance. Reading some of the more alarmist literature, you would be forgiven thinking that the decision-making process of the Belt and Road is like the war room in Stanley Kubrick's *Dr Strangelove*. In this vision, depicted in elaborate maps with colourful lines that resemble the tentacles of the "communist octopus", Chinese tankers conquer the world's oceans, ports acquired by Chinese companies are turned into naval bases for the People's Liberation Army (PLA), while Chinese products, companies, associations and individuals armed with briefcases full of cash are assumed to be the soldiers, missiles and tanks invading any country they can. At times it seemed that some western commentators could only talk about China using Cold War stereotypes and dragon metaphors, sometimes with a sprinkling of "yellow peril" racism. Yet the Belt and Road functions much like any Chinese policy: the centre provides the narrative, the incentives and the red lines, and various other actors jockey to improve their relative position in the system by pitching their own versions and contributing their own policy implementation work.

Because the flow of information is never foolproof (unintentionally or by design), and the interests of different actors never perfectly aligned, there will inevitably be misalignment between the wishes of the centre and the implementation on the ground. The BRI is different in that it involves international as well as domestic actors, state enterprises, private companies and local governments in both China and host nations, meaning its complexity as a policy can only increase. Ignoring the contradictions inherent in such a multifarious decision-making environment and reducing them to a single design cannot be the foundation of our knowledge about it.

Third, the perception of the BRI as a "global domination" project overshadows a whole range of issues that are of grave importance for our societies and economies. When we fret that the presence of China Ocean Shipping Company (COSCO) in Piraeus is the present-day equivalent of the British colonizing Malta, why should we even bother about anything else, including environmental degradation, labour rights, operational efficiency, transparency and integrity, or the planned expansion of the port that coastal communities fiercely and successfully opposed? When national security concerns triumph over all other issues, the tendency to talk about Chinese companies as tentacles of the Chinese Communist Party (CCP) deprioritizes concerns that are much more tangible, immediate and impactful on our lives. Essentializing the BRI leads us not only to simplistic conclusions but diverts our attention away from what matters to local societies and economies.

Lastly, this logic sustains a yawning perception gap between China and the world, which both CCP propagandists and hawkish "China Threat" advocates in the West are quick to fill. Just as the former fill the air with stories of "mutual benefit and win-win cooperation" (*huli gongying* 互利共赢), so the latter talk about debt traps and Trojan horses (Heath & Gray 2018). As there is limited common understanding of what the BRI is, public debate is captured either by saccharine propaganda or bitter accusations. In turn, this perception-based debate and the complacent explanations it offers sustain the vacuum of knowledge exchange and debate in a self-reinforcing manner. With no scope for debate between the CCP's win-win propaganda and the dragon tales of China Threat advocates, there is a clear need for fact-based analyses to inform the public debate.

Fortunately, many researchers around the world have been working precisely on that, using approaches that vary from grounded empirical research to theoretical debates and global histories. This book is, therefore, intended as an effort to understand the BRI based on solid academic research, not perceptions or discourse. To achieve that, we rely on our own research and the rich body of academic literature, which, regrettably, is often inaccessible to the public. Although scholars have unearthed the complex realities of the BRI, academic research is designed to be communicated to peers with institutional access to academic depositories "guarded" as heavily as gold reserves behind unaffordable paywalls or expensive academic publications intended for libraries. University-based research that documents the convoluted decision-making process and developmental trajectory of the BRI is thereby often sidelined by polarized discourses that serve political agendas and reflect pre-existing biases.

Our aim is twofold: to communicate some of the key findings of the BRI-related scholarly literature to the informed public, and produce a narrative that appreciates nuance and complexity and advances the academic discussion on the topic. In a debate captured by the loud voices of CCP propagandists and China Threat advocates, we hope to offer a concise, informative and thought-provoking account that will highlight the BRI's origins, driving forces, contradictions, serious challenges and the opportunities it creates.

WHY DOES THE BRI MATTER?

Making sense of the BRI and its importance is not an easy endeavour. Our sceptical attitude towards propaganda slogans and hawkish alarmism recognizes the ambiguities that can frustrate attempts to interpret China's motives. Therefore, we first asked ourselves why the BRI matters to China and what that might tell us about the Initiative itself. Xi Jinping, China's ambitious leader since late 2012, is in particular tied to the Initiative as its author and patron, having first announced it shortly after his ascension to the position of General Secretary of the CCP. As such, the BRI is often seen as a symbol of China's new-found activism and desire for global recognition, replacing the cautious diplomatic stance of Deng Xiaoping, who advocated in favour of keeping a "low profile" in international affairs (Brown 2018: 79–80).

Although the BRI is associated with Xi Jinping, he curiously has few formal functions regarding the overseeing of the Initiative, which is entrusted to Vice-Premier Han Zheng and a group of economic bureaucracies (Manuel 2019). On the other hand, the BRI was inscribed into the CCP's constitution at its 19th Party congress in 2017, giving it a formal prominence that has not been accorded to many other foreign policy slogans (Brown 2022: 185). Xi, while not presiding over the daily operations of the BRI, is nonetheless strongly associated with the Initiative and has, for example, replaced Premier Li Keqiang as the host of the 17+1 network of China and Central and Eastern European states, a key subgrouping of the BRI. This means that the BRI has significant political capital for Xi and other Chinese leaders, which is a first step in unpacking its importance.

Second, the BRI greatly matters for China's foreign relations. Combining industrial policy, trade policy, elements of developmental aid and geostrategic considerations, the BRI is at home in several policy categories. Development and shared prosperity are the Initiative's stated offerings to the world, but these "gifts" are not always well received because China's motives appear unclear. The startling scope of the BRI alone, spanning 145 countries across the globe, has given rise to apprehension and anxiety in those already wary of China, such as the US, Australia, Japan and India. China's increased activism has caused consternation even in traditionally more sympathetic places. In Myanmar, local resistance to Chinese infrastructure projects such as the Myitsone dam increasingly defines relations between the two countries. Even in Pakistan, China's oldest ally, a member of former Prime Minister Imran Khan's cabinet expressed his dismay about benefits accruing mainly to Chinese companies rather than to Pakistan (Anderlini, Sender & Bokhari 2018). The BRI is already having a direct impact on China's relations with the world and especially with its neighbours. Moreover, the way regional organizations, national governments, local officials, businesses and civil society understand the BRI will inform their engagement with China and Chinese actors in multiple fields.

Third, we can make sense of the large and fluid initiative by way of comparison. The BRI has frequently been measured against the Marshall

Plan and the Bretton Woods system, which enabled the US to rise as the main security provider of the West and as the epicentre of global capitalism. It comes as no surprise, therefore, that in our quest to understand the nature, design and impact of the BRI, many people have drawn parallels between China's rise and that of the US after the Second World War. There is no doubt that money buys political influence, but the BRI is not a Marshall Plan. In 1948, following the devastation of world war, the US financed the economic development of its European allies to curb the influence of domestic communist parties and the strategic advancement of the Soviet Union (Kunz 1997). The Marshall Plan had an antagonistic orientation from its outset, concentrating on 16 European countries and excluding those under Soviet occupation and influence. As such, the Marshall Plan was a key precursor of the Euro-Atlantic security architecture and was indeed followed a year later by the creation of the North Atlantic Treaty Organization (NATO). It is therefore not surprising that the Marshall Plan took mainly the form of state aid through grants, not loans, with the former consisting 90 per cent of the approximate US$12.5 billion (equivalent to $135 billion in 2020 dollars according to the US Bureau of Labour Consumer Price Index) spent between 1948 and 1951 (Tarnoff 2018: 10–11). The Marshall Plan was an organized and institutionalized endeavour, with a clear strategic logic, geographical scope and duration, supplemented by strong security arrangements.

In the case of the BRI, even the most fervent supporters of China Threat theories struggle to identify a unified strategic rationale. The BRI is not antagonistic in design, it imposes no geopolitical exclusions or "camps" and has no clear security agenda attached to it. Of course, it creates economic competition within a global economic context by benefiting Chinese business actors and it has also increased the anxiety of countries such as India that feel the BRI encroaches on their sphere of influence. However, straight from its outset, the BRI had an economic and developmental rationale that was reflected in its institutional ecosystem at the central level. The head of its coordinating body, the BRI-Leading Small Group (LSG), is a vice-premier, while the participating organizations do not include the PLA or any other security apparatuses (Manuel 2019). In addition, there has been no spill-over in the realm of security yet; the economic activities of Chinese companies ("win-win" or not) have not led to the creation of new bilateral or collective military formations, although BRI projects often dovetail existing security links, such as those with central Asian autocracies and Pakistan.

Similarly, a careful comparison between China's financial institutions and the Bretton Woods system demonstrates that the BRI is far less ambitious and influential. Let us take the example of the Asian Infrastructure Investment Bank (AIIB), China's contribution to the club of multilateral development banks (MDBs). The AIIB is often seen as part of a grand design, an emblem of China's rise and the frontline of normative competition that will undermine the existing world order (Mirski 2014). Its decision in 2020 to make an emergency loan to China as part of the efforts to combat the Covid-19 pandemic similarly raised some eyebrows, but the AIIB's importance lies primarily in how unremarkable its existence has been so far.

The bank stands out in three ways: its commitment to physical infrastructure, its insistence of non-interference in host-state political order, and the high voting share attributed to China (26.6 per cent), which enables it to block any decisions requiring a supermajority. However, rather than create an alternative to the Bretton Woods institutions, the AIIB seems to be complementing them. Capitalized at $100 billion with $19 billion paid-in capital, the bank counted 103 member states, 53 of which are non-regional (non-Asian) countries. By the end of 2021 it had cumulatively approved $31.97 billion in financing – a comparatively modest amount. More importantly, however, the AIIB has expanded its cooperation with the World Bank, the Asian Development Bank and the European Bank for Reconstruction and Development, and as a result many recent projects are co-financed rather than standalone. The AIIB is closely integrated into global developmental finance, and all co-financed projects must adhere to the rules set by co-funding bodies. Instead of an instrument of global domination, the AIIB is rapidly evolving to be a part of the global development finance architecture.

Although the BRI is different to both the Marshall Plan and the Bretton Woods system, we need to recognize that economic interests create political ones, especially when projects involve state-owned enterprises (SOEs) and are financed by state banks, such as China Export-Import Bank (China Exim) or the China Development Bank (CDB). China's attempt to increase its global economic footprint will inevitably lead to a more recognized international standing, a more active role in security and greater diplomatic weight. However, the still uncertain geopolitical gains of the BRI are more of a welcomed side-effect for the CCP rather than an underlying logic, as was the case with the Marshall Plan and the US-centred financial architecture of Bretton Woods. Indeed, as the BRI matured over the last decade, profitability and economic sustainability became of increasing importance to the Chinese government's BRI balance sheet (Shen & Zhang 2018), especially when grand geostrategic designs that were included under the BRI umbrella, such as the China–Pakistan Economic Corridor (CPEC), failed to deliver the expected results.

If security priorities are not the main driver for the BRI, then what is? To answer this question, we first approach the BRI as an initiative focused on SOEs operating in the infrastructural sectors, from construction to energy and logistics. In the 2017 Belt and Road Forum, Xi described it as the "project of the century", as "a partnership ... of friendship rather than an alliance", promoting the idea that "infrastructural connectivity is the foundation of development" (Xi 2017). In the keynote speech to the 2nd BRI in 2019, Xi Jinping reiterated that "connectivity is vital to advancing Belt and Road cooperation" and that "infrastructure is the bedrock of connectivity" (Xi 2019).

Even the AIIB differs from its peers, mainly in its exclusive emphasis on lending to infrastructure projects. But the construction, operation and integration of physical and regulatory connectivity in the form of infrastructural and logistical projects also extends features of the Chinese political and economic system outward, where they interact with those of host states. The BRI on the ground often takes the form of Chinese companies building and operating global infrastructure financed by Chinese state capital; that is, it extends the ecosystem of Chinese state capitalism.

China's emphasis on physical and regulatory infrastructure chimes with Organisation for Economic Co-operation and Development (OECD) estimates of a global infrastructural gap, estimated at $6.3 trillion annually between 2016 and 2030 for a total of $95 trillion. Although no official number exists, China's total BRI commitments are estimated at up to $1.3 trillion (Rolland 2019b). Actual lending levels are hard to ascertain but the grand total of all loans underwritten by the China Export and Credit Insurance Corporation (Sinosure) in 2015, $570.56 billion, is a good proxy number (OECD 2018: 19). A report co-written by the People's Bank of China and the City of London corporation meanwhile claims a total of 1,485 projects worth $837.41 billion were launched by 2018 (CLC 2018: 5). This does not mean China has invested nearly a trillion dollars on the world's development, however. Many of the projects do not have a clear developmental value and are, moreover, financed by a mixture of concessional and commercial loans, paid ultimately by the host states themselves. Yet despite this, China is providing a type of "public service". The infrastructural gap exists, and western financing (multilateral or commercial) has not provided sufficient funds so far, especially in riskier jurisdictions where infrastructural investments can lead to big losses. Chinese finance cannot avoid those risks either, as Sinosure's $1 billion loss on a railroad project in Ethiopia demonstrated (Ng 2018).

To summarize, the BRI is a signature foreign policy of an ambitious leader, creating mixed reactions from friends and foes, but it is not China's Marshall Plan, nor does it have the geopolitical force and ambition to upend the liberal world order. More than a grand design, the BRI is about expanding the playing field for Chinese enterprise and capital, with all the consequences that this brings and that we explore in this book. On one hand, it marks a departure from the inward-looking diplomacy of Xi's predecessors. On the other, it is, nevertheless, a foreign policy initiative driven by the needs of the domestic economy. Despite this ambiguity of its political nature, what is certain is that the BRI has already become too big to fail. So long as Xi Jinping's authority is secure, success of the BRI will be guaranteed in one form or another, even through the long hiatus of the Covid-19 pandemic.

As the Initiative completes its first decade in 2023, there will undoubtedly be a rethinking of some of the riskier practices. Already, Xi has announced an end to overseas coal projects and many reckless private actors have been excised from the BRI's portfolio. That in itself is indicative of how the BRI will continue to play a key role in China's foreign policy: as a label that brings together the many disparate aspects of Global China.

OUR APPROACH

We are both political scientists with a track record of studying Chinese policy and government, so we did not approach the BRI like an international relations phenomenon, but saw it primarily as a CCP policy. This is why we proceeded to study it as we would any key CCP policy: by understanding the party's own narrative and propaganda, by looking at implementation and the hierarchies through which the policy must pass and by identifying key actors that have varying access to power and therefore shape the policy in different ways. This led us to believe that the BRI is best analyzed as a platform designed to promote the global profit-seeking activities of Chinese SOEs and to address the People's Republic of China's (PRC's) long-term strategic needs, namely energy, resource and food security, through the creation of new lines of infrastructural and trade connectivity. While SOEs have a key role, the BRI reflects a wide range of interests in China's political and economic system: elite aims of CCP survival and the building of a strong world power, provincial competition, private sector profit-seeking, to name but a few. Our understanding of the BRI emphasizes the interplay between two complex ecosystems: that of China's state capitalism and those of host countries.

Regarding the first, we view the BRI fundamentally as an extension of China's experience with development. The political and economic statecraft that underpins it is characterized by a top-down, statist logic of central planning that, nevertheless, encourages and relies on the initiative and experimentation of a multitude of state, non-state, central and local actors. While such experimentation has been a strength of the Chinese economic model, it has its drawbacks: difficulties in implementation, varying capacity across government, tensions between priorities at different scales of government and turf wars, not to mention the increased opportunities for malfeasance. The BRI, although overtly a foreign policy initiative, must contend with similar dynamics and satisfy many different needs that exist *inside* China's political and economic elites. SOEs try to get the state's attention and financial backing for their often-opportunistic investments, local governments compete to be included in BRI cash flows, and private enterprises have attempted to label their expansion plans as part of the initiative – sometimes to the chagrin of the CCP. Therefore, an analytical approach to the BRI requires us to explore the drivers behind this policy initiative in the context of Chinese economic statecraft.

However, although the ideas, motives and (most of) the money involved in the BRI comes from China, the development and outcome of specific projects is determined locally, in host countries. Therefore, the second important source of complexity we focus on is the interaction between Chinese and local actors, who are engaged in a risky and often unpredictable dance of implementation and experimentation characterized by a multitude of agendas and considerable information gaps. So, whereas the CCP can set the tune domestically, this is often much more difficult on a transnational scale, where host governments, local state authorities, business interests and societal actors create a perplexing ecosystem of investment. Chinese companies are sometimes presented as the modern-day equivalent of colonial entities, a view that downgrades the agency of host states and casts local actors as passive supplicants at the mercy of Chinese cash. A closer examination shows that the simplicity of the "bad investors–weak hosts" prism undermines our understanding of the BRI's development, and of the factors behind the success or failure of many projects.

Taking all this into account, it is clear that key protagonists of the BRI, such as Chinese SOEs, face complexity at home and uncertainty abroad. They must navigate through the multifarious decision-making processes of state capitalism so that they can find themselves in the uncharted waters of host-state business environments. Partly the product of design and partly of expediency, the BRI's complexity is its defining characteristic. It is one thing to identify motives and another to explain its developmental trajectory. If we mistake one for the other, we will end up creating narratives that may grab the public's attention but not grasp the reality of the BRI.

Elsewhere, we have discussed how the public perception of the BRI is shaped by China Threat advocates who propagate alarmist narratives even when supporting evidence is scant (Rogelja & Tsimonis 2020). Having said that, there are many justified grounds for criticism against the CCP: its abysmal record of human rights abuse that has deteriorated under Xi Jinping, the intensified suppression of civil society, the horrors taking place in Xinjiang, the many unanswered questions over its handling of the pandemic, and the regime's refusal to comply with calls for transparency at home and abroad. Threat discourses and authoritarian practices have created a difficult context of reference for cool-headed approaches to anything relating to China.

As we demonstrate in the subsequent chapters, some features of China's authoritarian space do travel along the Initiative's routes and countries that vocally opposed the CCP's domestic policies were quickly shut out from the presumed benefits of the BRI. But the Initiative's high visibility is as much a reputational problem for China as it is a weapon of coercive diplomacy. In this book, we unpack the BRI's complexity and suggest ways of thinking about it that, we hope, will allow the reader to appreciate its different dimensions and aspects in a fair and non-essentializing manner.

QUESTIONS AND OUTLINE

We have organized this book around a series of questions that we often get asked about the BRI and to which we ourselves wanted to provide clear answers wherever possible. In addition, we canvassed opinion and solicited questions from our immediate and extended professional networks to find out what practitioners in the field most often want to know about the Initiative. To our surprise, rather than big questions about China's rise or American decline, the queries were practical: When did the BRI begin? Which countries does it involve? Who are the key players? How does it compare to previous similar initiatives? Given that Chinese companies have been investing abroad for decades now, what is new about it? Are BRI projects sustainable or do they replicate China's own problematic experience of environmentally and socially damaging development? How transparent and fair are the deals involving Chinese SOEs? Can western businesses take part in the initiative? We organized these and other questions into five sections: the basics of state capitalism, the global politics of the BRI, its environmental sustainability, its transparency and integrity, and its social impact.

The second chapter addresses the basic aspects of the BRI (milestones, scope, organization) and links it with the globalization of China's state capitalism. We explain the BRI as the continuation of Beijing's previous similar efforts and initiatives to support the internationalization of Chinese companies as we consider the role of state capitalism in the

Initiative. We then examine its decision-making ecosystem and sketch out the profile of key political (government, banks and the party) and business actors (SOEs, private companies, hybrids). By comparing the BRI with previous state-backed efforts and by mapping its internal organization, we assess change and continuity in the government's motives and goals, and prepare the reader for the analysis in the following chapters.

Chapter 3 asks whether the Belt and Road is an attempt to reshape the world into a Sinocentric form. Many established explanations of the BRI view it as a challenge to the existing global order, a view that reduces the activities of Chinese actors to the will of the CCP, or even just of Xi Jinping. In a country where the will of the CCP pervades business and social life, it is indeed difficult to find nuance – yet this makes it even more important. Despite its magnitude, the BRI does not have the organizational, normative and ideological clarity to act as a foundation of a new world order. Although we doubt its hegemonic credentials, we emphasize that China has identified a demand for conditionality-free loans that are in turn weakening the leverage of western players.

Chapter 4 addresses the issue of sustainability. China's importance in creating a sustainable world future is undeniable, with the BRI bearing relevance on all 17 of the United Nations' (UN's) sustainable development goals. But how sustainable is China's own globalization? What are the concerns in terms of the effect on environmental standards and the lives of local communities? The chapter focuses on using environmental protection to evaluate the commitment of the BRI to equitable and sustainable development. China's own economic model since 1978 has been markedly environmentally destructive, prompting widespread scepticism about the intentions (and capabilities) of Chinese firms abroad. The chapter will evaluate the impact of existing practices on creating a downward pressure on protective regulation in BRI projects and the prospects for materializing a "green future for the Initiative", as per Xi Jinping's 2019 pledge.

The fifth chapter concentrates on issues of integrity and transparency. The increasing international presence of Chinese companies has fostered apprehension globally on the fairness of their business conduct. China's domestic business environment has long been characterized by a great deal of "informality", practices that are based on the logic of interpersonal relations and exchange (*guanxi*), under-the-table transactions between state officials and private companies to gain competitive advantages, and collusion. Graft, B2B corruption and practices oriented towards limiting competition have long been regarded as a trademark of "doing business in China". With these observations in mind, this chapter will assess whether Chinese companies and banks create "a Belt and a Road of corruption", promoting business practices that are characterized by lack of transparency and poor corporate governance.

Chapter 6 looks at what other direct impacts the BRI has had on local communities. We examine how China's understanding of human rights rests on a rigid sovereigntist logic that has in the past allowed it to both ignore genocidal tendencies in its allies such as Sudan, as well as resist any foreign "meddling" in its domestic mechanisms of oppression. The BRI replicates this logic, both indirectly and directly. The Initiative's social impact is perhaps most obvious in the area of labour rights. As a transnational network of infrastructural projects, the BRI reflects and reproduces structural inequalities that are the hallmark of many a construction site. Some labour violations stem from the weakness of host-state labour regimes, while others are attributable to the actions of unscrupulous intermediaries supplying the Initiative's sites with cheap labour, often in the form of posted (dispatch) workers from the Global South.

We conclude with a reflection on our findings and link them with current developments in the era of new global anxieties, with Russia's invasion of Ukraine coming hot on the heels of a global pandemic that has transformed China into a closed country. We suggest, with a dash of optimism, that China's economic slowdown might open opportunities for more equitable collaboration, thereby allowing non-Chinese actors to shape the BRI's future development and direction. As the CCP begins to tally the score of the BRI's first decade, it will want to present it as the lean, clean and green initiative of Xi's speeches. By pointing out its actual shortcomings – and not scaremongering about a new world order – the global community will be able to encourage Chinese actors to take stock of the reactions the BRI has engendered. There are early indications of this in Chinese academic debate and we can only hope their counsel reaches the halls of Zhongnanhai. The more high-profile a global policy initiative is, the more leverage other stakeholders have, which is why we hope our effort will contribute to an informed debate that might yet deliver on some of the vaunted opportunities of China's global ambition.

2

How is the BRI organized?

Many analysts have noted that the BRI is missing a map (Narins & Agnew 2020). This is puzzling because mapping is commonly used by the CCP to reshape geopolitical realities according to its nationalistic and strategic priorities: depicting Taiwan as a province, laying claim to the entire South China Sea with the infamous "9 dash-line", delineating China's Exclusive Economic Zone and claiming sovereignty over the Senkaku/Diaoyutai islands are just the most recent examples of mapping as a way to define where China begins and ends. In addition, maps have been employed to graphically correct historical "mistakes" in China's borders with Vietnam, India and Russia, while today nationalistic circles refer to (ironically western) maps of the Qing dynasty as part of their nostalgia for a time when China ruled all under heaven. Given the systematic use of maps to imagine China in the world and vis-à-vis its neighbours, why is there not an official, definitive map of the BRI? The answer lies in the BRI's gradual evolution from a development initiative on China's periphery to its main global platform for economic relations and diplomacy.

The official narrative states that the BRI was initiated in September 2013, when Xi Jinping publicly promoted the creation of a "Silk Road Economic Belt" with central Asian nations while on an official visit in Astana, Kazakhstan. The following month, he made a similar announcement from Jakarta, calling for a twenty-first-century "Maritime Silk Road" of investment and trade. The Belt and Road appeared for the first time in an official party policy document in November 2013, where setting up new financial institutions and improving infrastructural connectivity with neighbouring countries are stated as aims of the Silk Road Economic Belt and the Maritime Silk Road (Communist Party of China 2013). Its debut in the realm of policy documents was a modest one, given the BRI's subsequent development. The reference to what would evolve into the BRI was hidden at the end of point 26 of China's plans for deepening reform in a paragraph titled "Further opening up inland and border areas".

But the idea gained a lot of momentum in 2014 because Xi Jinping continued to tirelessly promote it in international forums. The BRI was included in the government's annual work report and began to appear as a separate policy subject in CCP documents. In February 2015, the party established the BRI "Small Leading Group", a semi-formal but very important institution for policy-making that signified its elevation from the realm of abstract rhetoric to a priority policy area. A month later, the State Council published its "Vision and Actions on Jointly Building Silk Road Economic Belt and 21st Century Maritime Silk Road", in which it outlined its understanding of the project. The "Vision" significantly expanded the scope of the BRI, from Southeast and Central Asia to the entire Asian, European and African continents. It also provided a clearer picture of its ambitions, "promoting peace, development, cooperation and mutual benefit" in the context of a world recovering from the 2008 financial crisis that is moving towards multipolarity.

Some of the rhetoric was not new, as China's relations with the developing world, and in particular Africa, have shown a remarkable consistency stretching back to the Maoist period (Strauss 2009). But Xi's vision explained the BRI as a "systematic project", identifying the main components of its framework: the Silk Road Economic Belt routes linking China with (1) Central Asia, Russia and the Baltic; (2) the Persian Gulf and the Mediterranean Sea through Central and West Asia; and (3) the Southeast Asia, South Asia and the Indian Ocean. The Twenty-First-Century Maritime Silk Road extends westwards from China to Europe through the South China Sea and the Indian Ocean, and eastwards to the South Pacific. With strong support by Xi Jinping himself, a leading coordination mechanism and a delineated vision, the BRI was now ready to take off.

The establishment of China's Silk Road Fund in 2014 and, most importantly, the creation of the AIIB in 2016, showcased China's financial commitment and provided the basis for further institutionalization and expansion. The AIIB gained the endorsement of key G7 countries and many advanced economies, as China skilfully pursued an agenda of inclusion and shared interests rather than exclusion and antagonism to western-led institutions (Knoerich & Urdinez 2019). China ensured that AIIB members would be able to exert influence on the bank's decision-making and pursue business opportunities as equals (*ibid.*: 349). The mass entry of numerous western advanced economies showcases the non-hegemonic nature of the AIIB that has been a key element of its success in this early stage of its establishment. The AIIB continues to act as a smart, multilateral cover that attracts a lot of attention, but it is by no means the key funder of the BRI. For all the anger it set off in Washington, their ire would have been better directed at China's policy banks that bankroll most of the BRI's projects.

Alongside the AIIB, China expanded its diplomatic initiatives through multilateral and bilateral forums on economic cooperation. The first groupings included the Forum on China–Africa Cooperation (FOCAC) and the "16+1" (Cooperation between China and Central and Eastern European Countries, briefly 17+1 and 14+1 since August 2022), alongside new initiatives, such as the China–CELAC Forum (China and Community of Latin American and Caribbean States), and created a new layer of asymmetric multilateralism that promotes Chinese interests and investments into every part of the world. At a bilateral level there is a proliferation of memoranda of understanding (MoUs) and cooperation agreements from Peru to Pakistan and from Kenya to Italy.

The most important global diplomatic initiative is the BRI Forum for International Cooperation (FIC), held in 2017 and 2019, which brought together more than 130 countries and close to 40 heads of state and government. The FIC is in its initial stage of institutional formation but is developing into a nascent multilateral cooperation mechanism. The FIC's Leadership Roundtable is the top-level organ for multilateral negotiations and agreements, while satellite thematic forums bring together CEOs, bureaucrats and think tanks to discuss and exchange ideas. The forum provides Chinese leaders the opportunity to share and test their plans and priorities for the BRI with a global audience. For instance, the 2019 forum sparked discussions over a "BRI 2.0", which would pay more attention to regulation, frameworks for good governance, environmental and social responsibility, as well as anti-corruption (see Ang 2019). These bilateral and multilateral diplomatic initiatives reflect the BRI's global scope.

The BRI has served as an umbrella for consolidating pre-existing projects and launching new ones. For instance, the CPEC, a series of investments enhancing economic, diplomatic and strategic cooperation between the two countries, was hailed in 2013 as one of the kick-starting projects of the BRI, but was actually under planning for some time. COSCO's investment in the Port of Piraeus, which started in 2008, gained momentum post-2013 and expanded significantly as it secured the strong financial and political support of the Chinese state. The Addis Ababa–Djibouti Railway was also initiated in 2011 but rebranded as a BRI project in subsequent years.

Since 2013, however, we have seen a considerable expansion of economic activities as Chinese companies rushed to identify opportunities abroad and take advantage of the BRI bonanza. These include a mix of investments and construction contracts; for instance, the acquisitions of Italian tyres manufacturer Pirelli by ChemChina, of Geneva-based Addax Petroleum by Sinopec, of Peru's Chaglla hydroelectric plant by Three Gorges, and the construction of the Abuja–Warri railway in Nigeria by China Railway Construction Corp International, and of the mega-shipyard King Salman International Complex in Saudi Arabia and the Teyo Tufanbeyli power station in Turkey by Power Construction Corporation of China (Power China).

One way to measure the scope and dynamics of the BRI is to look at the total amount of investment and construction contracts awarded to Chinese state-owned companies in countries that have subsequently signed MoUs on the BRI (Table 2.1). From a total yearly amount of $15.6 billion in 2005, total investment and contracts peaked in 2015 at $117 billion, then stabilized to around $100 billion annually before dropping precipitously in 2020 and 2021 (AEI 2022). This suggests there was already an upward (and outward) trend for Chinese enterprises to bid for business globally, but the BRI seems to have accelerated and magnified it. The drop in 2020/21 can largely be explained by the Covid-19 pandemic, although there were some signs of a tapering in outgoing loans even before, as Chinese lenders sought to consolidate existing problematic debts instead of pursuing new lending (Mingey & Kratz 2021).

The rise of the BRI's economic and diplomatic tides created significant political capital for Xi Jinping. Recognizing its importance for China's foreign affairs, the 19th Party Congress enshrined the BRI in CCP

Table 2.1 Investments by and construction contracts awarded to Chinese SOEs in 142 BRI countries, 2005–20.

Year	Investment and construction contracts (in US$ billions)
2005	15.620
2006	33.550
2007	30.450
2008	49.370
2009	52.980
2010	61.540
2011	78.260
2012	71.140
2013	88.060
2014	91.650
2015	117.870
2016	100.740
2017	96.890
2018	97.110
2019	100.290
2020	51.060

Source: China Global Investment Tracker, American Enterprise Institute 2022.

Note: The list of BRI countries is based on China's own calculation and includes some countries (such as Russia) who have neither confirmed nor denied the signing of an MoU on the BRI.

constitution: "[The Party] shall follow the principle of achieving shared growth through discussion and collaboration, and pursue the Belt and Road Initiative." This amendment is a testament to Xi's political dominance in the CCP but it also signalled to Chinese SOEs, local governments, the public and the world that the BRI is here to stay. As a result of the above, the BRI has evolved from an ambitious development initiative in its periphery to China's main engine for economic and diplomatic engagement with the world. The capital invested in it, both financial and political, renders it a flagship policy that simply cannot be seen to fail.

The seemingly open-ended and ever-evolving character of the BRI explains the lack of an official map but also reveals a rather complex process of development. In the present chapter of this effort to make sense of the BRI, we will introduce the basics, concentrating not on multibillion projects but on the Initiative's ecosystem and origin, on the key players involved and the ways they relate to one another. Our emphasis will be on the BRI's protagonists, the Chinese SOEs, and the many domestic and international challenges they face in pursuing profitable operations abroad.

THE BRI'S ECOSYSTEM: STATE CAPITALISM AND POLICY PREDECESSORS

China's state capitalist system is the product of a gradual and experimental approach, famously described by Deng Xiaoping as "crossing the river by feeling the stones", and there is no reason not to apply a similar framework to our understanding of how this peculiar ecosystem affects the BRI. While we have established that the BRI has no precise map or blueprint, it does have some identifiable goals. The construction of new infrastructural connectivities is an example of a stated goal, as are the deepening of people-to-people ties. Conversely, the export of industrial production overcapacities and the accompanying internationalization of state-owned construction giants are their unstated counterparts, as is the deepening of dependencies on China, especially in its immediate neighbourhood.

China's state capitalism is the "native environment" from which the BRI and its participating institutions and enterprises originate. The overwhelming presence of the state in China's economy is a unique trait not found among the world's major economies. While it is true that the state's share of the economy has declined significantly since the beginning of economic reforms, from practically 100 per cent to around 30 per cent of China's gross domestic product (GDP) (Zhang 2019), this statistic belies a more complex picture. This is because, despite this rebalancing, China's economy remains in many ways dominated by the state sector. Although dynamic and numerous, the vast majority of private enterprises are small to medium size, and many of them rely heavily on links with local party officials for survival (Kroeber 2016: 90). Even large private enterprises can be punished for stepping out of line, so smaller players can hardly be expected to have much say on economic policy. The case of CEFC China Energy (whose Czech dealings are discussed in the hierarchy and layering section below) is instructive: after an unsanctioned $9 billion deal to acquire a 14.7 per cent stake in Russian oil giant Rosneft, the company executive was arrested and the company nationalized (Paik 2021: 112).

The so-called "commanding heights" of the economy are controlled by the central state, and many levels of local government also operate province- or city-level state-owned enterprises. This poses certain problems for the state because it is simultaneously the owner, financier, insurer and regulator of the sector. In the context of the BRI, the state additionally becomes the SOEs' diplomatic sponsor and liaison with host-state authorities. The focus on the functioning and the mechanics of state capitalism is warranted because the BRI, much more than the domestic economy, is dominated by national champions that operate in the sectors that contribute the most to the initiative: construction, energy, telecommunications, logistics and transportation.

Moreover, our observation of SOE activities must account for the layered and variegated hierarchy of decision-making. Xi Jinping's leadership has brought about new trial regulation on standardizing the presence of the party in SOEs that may lead to closer monitoring and control (Communist Party of China 2019). The regulation does not bring anything drastically new and many stipulations, such as the prominence of party committees in SOEs, had already been observed as a matter of custom. Nevertheless, the direction of reform has shifted away from the professionalization of corporate governance typical of the Hu-Wen era (Heilmann 2005) and towards increased control by the party centre. The country's top enterprises are led by high-ranking party members who are often also members of the party's central committee, the grouping of elite CCP cadres whose careers are intimately tied with their party standing. But to be politically loyal and run an SOE into the ground is not a career-enhancing strategy, so even loyal party cadres must consider the profitability (or at least manageable losses) of their business. Equally, the party has become better at appointing cadres that are both politically loyal as well as competent – not only in the state sector, but even in the private sector, as the 2008 appointment of the CEO of Minsheng, a major private bank, shows (Naughton & Tsai 2015: 38).

Recent attempts at recentralization notwithstanding, China's state capitalism* has long been characterized by experimentation and decentralization. As the state's (sometimes failed) attempts to reform SOEs have shown, SOEs are neither lifeless levers of the party-state, nor are they truly independent enterprises in pursuit of profit maximization. This view of China's state capitalism highlights the autonomy and experimentation of actors on the ground, particularly in conjunction with host-state actors. In Myanmar, for example, China Power Investment Company pushed through a hated dam project in Myitsone in opposition to regulation and by ignoring the Chinese embassy in Yangon (Jones & Zou 2017). The ensuing fallout and suspension of the project was seen as a major setback for Sino-Myanmar relations that would have been avoided had the SOE not gone "off-script". Although reminiscent of a military chain of command in form, China's state capitalist system is far from static. By extension, the same logic of gradualism, experimentation, decentralization and tolerance of particularistic interests by semi-autonomous state actors has also paved the way for the BRI's emergence.

The BRI may be Xi Jinping's signature foreign policy but it is shaped by state capitalism and forms part of a rich and complex policy ecosystem. At its most basic level, the BRI can be understood as an attempt to leverage domestic industrial overcapacity in order to expand China's geo-economic reach through enhanced connectivity – and it is not the first such attempt. The BRI's predecessors come in two sets: first, there are industrial policies that have fed directly into the BRI, such as the Going Out strategy for internationalizing state-owned enterprises, or the Made in China 2025 policy of industrial upgrading, which we discuss below. Second, the BRI also builds on policies designed to alleviate China's geostrategic anxieties by ensuring secure trade and supply lines, pacifying the country and maintaining a benign neighbourhood.

The Going Out strategy (*Zouchuqu Zhanlüe* 走出去战略) was first introduced in 1999 as the "Go Global" plan and was ostensibly aimed at incentivizing and supporting Chinese enterprises (particularly state-owned ones) to seek out new markets and expand their operations internationally. With roots in what Zhang calls the "aid-contracting nexus" (2020), the Going Out strategy built on China's economic diplomacy and developmental ethos that stretches back to the Maoist period. Much like the BRI, the strategy aimed to kill two birds with one stone.

First, it intended to upgrade China's sluggish SOEs into globally competitive corporations. SOEs involved in construction contracting were the first to be allowed to operate globally (Hong & Sun 2006), followed by logistics and energy companies – a sectoral triad that still dominates the BRI. Responding to the policy, Chinese enterprises used their specific advantages when making investment decisions: risk mitigation, experience with developing markets and a large domestic market to fall back on. This enabled them to not shy away from riskier investment destinations (Buckley *et al.* 2007) and many SOEs used less-developed markets as springboards to gain experience – a characteristic that has endured into the BRI era (Rogelja 2020).

Second, the Going Out strategy aimed to tackle problems stemming from China's export-oriented economy, which generates huge capital flows. On one hand, large foreign exchange inflows can cause speculative bubbles or irrational investment. On the other hand, the Chinese government was also careful to not allow a premature outflow of capital from China, because its economic development model is hugely capital-intensive. In 1993, for example, the government decided to postpone support for SOEs' international activities (Liou 2009: 674), and it was not until 1999 that this idea returned in the guise of Going Out. Even today, striking a balance between international expansion and capital flight remains a priority for Chinese policymakers, and companies that anger the state can face swift retribution – as Dalian Wanda found out in 2017 (Clover & Ju 2017). The state maintains a careful watch on macroeconomic indicators and makes an example of firms (especially private) who engage in "irrational" investment that is seen as detrimental to the party's goals.

"Made in China 2025" is an industrial upgrading strategy announced in 2015 and aimed at upgrading China's manufacturing from low-tech, mass production to higher value-added sectors such as semiconductors, aerospace and biotech. The strategy is but one of a sequence of milestones (2025, 2035, 2049) that would result in China becoming a leading manufacturing power just in time for the centenary of the PRC's founding. The ambitious strategy caused concern in advanced manufacturing centres such as Germany and, in 2019, the CCP quietly dropped the slogan but kept the policy in place (Harada 2019).

Although the Made in China 2025 policy has a domestic focus, its goal aligns with some of the BRI's stated and unstated aims. The BRI is thus a part of a wider re-examination of China's developmental model, which since 1978 relied predominantly on becoming the world's factory. Export-led growth is now giving way to increased domestic consumption, which contributed nearly 60 per cent of its annual GDP growth in 2019 (National Bureau of Statistics of China 2020). The BRI is pivotal to these efforts as it simultaneously internationalizes China's largest firms, creates new export and import markets and provides the means to reach them.

Securing access to natural resources remains a key requirement for China's continued economic growth and is, therefore, at the heart of the BRI's *raison d'être* (Song 2015: 24). Despite policies aimed to foster domestic consumption, China is still very much the world's factory. It famously runs large trade surpluses with western economies but it also has large trade deficits with producers of specialized components and natural resources needed for manufacturing. The global footprint of China's economic development is usually expressed in its total GDP or aggregate trading volume, but its need to import natural resources is equally staggering. In 2019, China accounted for almost 70 per cent of the world's total import of iron ore, and close to 60 per cent of the total import of copper (ITC 2020). The demand for such imports is mainly motivated by China's export-oriented manufacturing industry, rather than domestic consumption or construction (Roberts & Rush 2012), meaning the raw materials that China imports form part of a complex production chain that stretches from consumers in industrialized economies to resource-rich developing countries.

The BRI as a globalized expression of China's industrial model may motivate Chinese enterprises to climb up the value chain, but it also aims to secure the existing supply of raw materials. As Gonzales-Vicente points out, the Chinese SOEs' acumen in building infrastructure in the developing world pairs well with investment in resource extraction – not because of an administrative fiat of the CCP, but because of the business decisions taken by firms themselves (Gonzalez-Vicente 2012). The BRI provides a sense of political cover and higher purpose to run-of-the-mill methods of securing resources, either direct negotiations with producing countries (e.g. through commodity-backed development loans), or the acquisition and investment into global mining assets (such as the 2018 deal by Tianqi Lithium to acquire a 25 per cent stake of Chile's SQM for $4.3 billion). Outward direct investment into resource extraction significantly pre-dates the announcement of the BRI, with the peak of outflows into extractive industries globally occurring between 2008 and 2010, in the wake of the global financial crisis: $29 billion in 2008, $27 billion in 2009 and $30.6 billion in 2010 (AEI 2022). The BRI has therefore not resulted in an increased appetite for the world's natural resources, as is sometimes suggested, but has instead provided a more coherent and normative basis from which Chinese SOEs can engage in global business.

Controlling resources at the site of production is, however, useless if they cannot safely and cheaply be brought back to China. Solving the Malacca dilemma has long been a bane of Chinese geostrategic planners. The Strait of Malacca, with its strategic position and calm seas, is a historic trade node and bottleneck for trade between East and South Asia. As China's economy became increasingly enmeshed into the world, so the Strait also came to be seen as China's Achilles' heel by many in the CCP. Although a wartime blockade by an enemy state is the worst-case scenario, Chinese policymakers are also concerned about the effects of congestion, piracy and terrorism on this chokepoint (Huang 2014: 11). Oil, accounting for a fifth of China's total primary energy supply (IEA 2020), is particularly vulnerable to disruptions in supply because as much as 85 per cent of China's supply has passed through the Strait of Malacca in the past years (Liu, Bao & Ou 2006: 79). The obvious solution to this issue is to construct alternative supply routes or boost energy self-sufficiency. Since the latter is predominantly a domestic challenge, we examine the search for alternative supply routes in this section. Broadly speaking, there are four new energy import corridors:

1. Russia–China gas pipelines such as the "Power of Siberia" line, a 3,000km line that cost around $60 billion to construct, or the oil-carrying Eastern Siberia–Pacific Ocean pipeline
2. The Kazakhstan–China oil pipeline and the Central Asia–China gas pipelines A, B, C and D (People's Map of Global China 2021)
3. Myanmar–China oil and gas pipelines linking the Kyaukpyu port to Yunnan province in China's southwest
4. CEPC linking the port of Gwadar on the coast of Pakistan with China's far west through pipelines and road haulage, although the feasibility of the pipeline is doubtful (Erickson & Collins 2010: 101).

All the alternative energy import routes come with their problems. Pipelines, unlike seaborne tankers, create lasting dependencies between the countries that use them – something Europe is painfully realizing as we write this. For China just as for Germany, pipelines will bring reliance on unstable regimes, the vagaries of Russia's geopolitical priorities and the risk of democratic processes undoing previously cosy relations between Beijing and the various autocracies in its vicinity.

The much-vaunted shortcut from the Persian Gulf to China via Pakistan is particularly fraught with risks. Writing in 2016, Mei Xinyu, a researcher at the Ministry of Commerce of the People's Republic of China (MOFCOM), wrote a polemic article suggesting the quest for alternative supply routes via Gwadar is bound to fail on both security and economic grounds. First of all, a pipeline (if it is even technically feasible) will never be as liquid an asset as a tanker. Mei calculates the cost of the pipeline is equal to commissioning 20 very large crude carriers with almost double the annual transport capacity as a pipeline (Mei 2016). On security issues, Mei dismisses the Malacca dilemma as a "bogus proposition", adding that the US navy would be perfectly capable of disrupting naval traffic into Gwadar, and that Pakistan's internal instability presents acute risks to any energy corridor (*ibid.*). As a geostrategic initiative to secure energy imports, the BRI has many such failings and shortcomings, and does a better job as a policy to support China's domestic enterprises and offer a vehicle for provincial diplomatic ambitions. Its effect is particularly visible in the borderlands of China, where it not only connects but also helps pacify China's rebellious western part.

The Great Western Development (GWD) strategy, also known as "Develop the West" or "Open Up the West" (*Xibu Dakaifa* 西部大开发) was announced in 1999 and hoped to bring the fruits of economic development, which had hitherto accrued mainly to the eastern coastal regions, to China's expansive western regions. The campaign grew to target 12 western provinces and neighbouring sub-provincial areas and was an early indicator of a shift of developmental policy from market-based mechanisms to renewed activism by the state (Goodman 2004: 318).

The GWD shares some important features with the BRI as a centrally driven developmental strategy aimed at creating synergies across provincial and national borders (Zhao 2016: 26). Like the BRI, the GWD was housed within the National Development and Reform Commission (NDRC), then called the State Development Planning Commission, and guided by a dedicated leading small group (Holbig 2004: 345). Like the BRI, it was an ambitious platform policy designed to mobilize various actors of the state economy on central and provincial levels. And, like the BRI, the GWD had a clear international aspect against the backdrop of China's World Trade Organization (WTO) entry (*ibid.*: 342). But, equally, the GWD campaign consisted not so much of brand-new funding and projects, but rather provided a banner under which many existing policies, projects and plans could be incorporated. In many ways it strengthened previous tendencies and processes by more tightly binding the resource-rich west to the industrial centres of coastal China (Oakes 2004). While the centre set the tone, the implementation was a "dynamic interaction" (Holbig 2004: 344–5) between central and subnational actors such as SOEs, provinces and municipalities.

In other ways, however, the GWD has deeper roots in centralized efforts to Sinicize China's west. In the case of Xinjiang, a predominately Muslim province, this effort dates back to late nineteenth-century Qing China policies (Millward 2007: 124). Compared to these early efforts of colonial expansion, the GWD differs in its "double" connectivity, linking Xinjiang (and Tibet) back to China as well as onwards to Central Asia and beyond (Clarke 2011: 149), a feature that has been inherited by the land-based part of the BRI.

The links to Central Asia go beyond physical infrastructure. After 9/11, the Chinese state successfully recast Uyghur separatism as part of a globalized Islamic terror. On the basis of this, China has cultivated security links to the various central Asian autocracies through initiatives such as the "Rapid Anti-terrorism Structure" in Tashkent (Sheives 2006: 213). It is hardly a coincidence that the BRI was first announced by Xi during a speech at Nazarbayev University in Kazakhstan's capital. The stability of the highly securitized border regions of China's west relies on the stability of the wider region. Having had success with a mixture of authoritarianism and economic development, China was eager to apply the same principles to Xinjiang through the GWD strategy (Becquelin 2004: 360). But economic development brought with it increased migration by Han Chinese, which in turn inflamed relations between the Uyghurs and the Chinese state. As infrastructural connectivities across China's borders bring further Han migration into Central Asia, so too have ethnic tensions and resentments been successfully exported. Anti-Chinese protest has become a regular occurrence in Kazakhstan, most recently in March 2021 when anti-regime groups organized a demonstration against "Chinese expansion" (Goble 2019; Radio Free Europe 2021).

The GWD campaign thus contributed to the BRI in terms of institutional design (being a platform rather than a clear policy with identifiable aims), the linking of domestic economic actors with the international environment, the space given to subnational actors, but also as an initiative aimed at consolidating Beijing's control of its borderlands. Like the BRI, it was closely linked to a leading political figure (Jiang Zemin) but was taken up by different actors with various goals, resulting sometimes in dissonant or layered policies. This is why we want to look at the multitude of actors shaping the BRI next, in order to understand their different power, roles and motives.

WHO'S WHO

Since the Belt and Road was launched in 2013, a whole range of terms and acronyms have found their way in the global public debate. These include the BRI's own variations as "Silk Road" and "OBOR" (One Belt, One Road – the initial official translation until the CCP introduced "BRI" in 2015), new international institutions such as the AIIB, forums such as the China-CEEC (Cooperation between China and Central and Eastern European Countries), but also Chinese state organizations, such as the NDRC and the SASAC (State-owned Asset Supervision and Administration Commission). The fast pace of the BRI's evolution left journalists, analysts and international businesses struggling to understand the cryptic-by-design institutional backbone of China's national development policy that has now acquired a global reach. Never before have internal Chinese party-state decisions mattered so much internationally, so there is a justified interest in understanding what these organizations do, how they operate and decide, and what their role and significance are in this opaque decision-making system. In this section, we will briefly introduce the most important actors and organizations involved in the BRI.

Xi Jinping and individual leaders

Would the BRI exist without Xi Jinping? Probably not. Although this question is important to understand the BRI's nature, it is actually impossible to answer it unequivocally. Nevertheless, it directs our attention to the key role Xi Jinping has played in creating the necessary momentum for the BRI to be endorsed and prioritized by substantial numbers of actors involved in its implementation. The BRI was Xi Jinping's second key policy following his famous anti-corruption campaign that was launched almost immediately after assuming office in late 2012. In many ways, the anti-corruption campaign and the BRI have a common ideological denominator, Xi Jinping's "China Dream". The China Dream is not just a slogan filled with emotion and pride for China's achievements so far but is a vision for the immediate future. According to this vision, the CCP, as a morally incorruptible and effective ruler, will lead Chinese society to prosperity and China to world greatness. Xi Jinping was instrumental in pursuing all these policies, so they have come to be closely identified with him.

As Xi moved rapidly to consolidate power by imposing discipline and purging enemies in the party, he simultaneously promoted the China Dream vision and the idea that would evolve into the BRI, both domestically and internationally. During his first year in office (2013), he was the main driver of the BRI but, as his power rapidly solidified, the BRI became part of the party's canon, encouraging new policies and institutions to support it. As the Initiative has become more institutionalized, other top-ranking cadres and members of the Politburo's Standing Committee (the leading organ of the CCP currently comprised of seven members), have been assigned important BRI tasks both internally and internationally. For instance, the BRI LSG (introduced below), in both its 2015 and 2018 composition, has been headed by a member of the Politburo Standing Committee, Zhang Gaoli and Han Zheng, respectively, while the China-CEEC is led by Premier Li Keqiang. The continuing public involvement of Xi Jinping and other Chinese leaders signifies that the BRI remains a policy priority for the CCP even as the Covid-19 pandemic has reduced the physical interaction between China and the world.

Leading Small Group for Promoting the Construction of the BRI (LSG)

The LSG is the equivalent to an inter-ministerial task force but it is one that brings together party as well as state leaders and is more institutionalized than ad hoc groups. As an institution it has deep roots in China's communist policy-making thinking and organization going back to 1958 (Miller 2008) when the CCP created LSGs to coordinate the implementation of domestic political campaigns. Since the reforms, faced with the task of coordinating many party committees, ministries, functional bureaucracies and state agencies, communist leaders created LSGs as a semi-formal institution that brings together leading cadres to discuss and coordinate the implementation of policies within the party-state. Accordingly, the CCP has set up LSGs to coordinate policy in the realms of national economy and development, foreign affairs and defence, politics and law, propaganda and ideology, Taiwan, Macao and Hong Kong affairs, among others (Miller 2008).

The BRI LSG was established under the State Council in 2015 and brings together key CCP leaders and technocrats. The BRI LSG is headed by Han Zheng, who is a member of the Politburo Standing Committee and the first vice-premier of the State Council (China's cabinet). Its other members include the head of the NDRC, the Director of the Office of the Central Foreign Affairs Committee of the CCP, the Vice-Premier of the State Council, the Secretary-General of the State Council and leading officials from development banks, and ministries and state agencies in economy, finance and foreign affairs. The composition of this LSG reveals the primacy of economic development concerns and it has no representation by the PLA (Manuel 2019), which is normally involved in LSGs with a security dimension such as the Taiwan affairs group.

National Development Reform Commission (NDRC)

Nicknamed the "Ministry of Ministries" or the "Little State Council" (Zhang 2014), the NDRC and its predecessors have been at the centre of national economic development policy since 1988. With 26 functional departments and 890 members of staff, its functions cover a comprehensive range of primarily macroeconomic and regulatory issues, including a role in fiscal, monetary, land, outbound investment and price policies.

The NDRC's involvement in the BRI stems from its long experience with regional development in both affluent and underdeveloped parts of China.

As we elaborate in the following section, the BRI in many ways builds on China's experience of promoting regional development; as such it should come as no surprise that the NDRC is considered to be its core organ. Indeed, organizationally, the NDRC hosts the Office of the Leading Group for Promoting the Construction of the BRI, alongside other small leading groups focusing on the development of the western region, the revitalization of Northeast China and of other old industrial bases, and the Beijing–Tianjin–Hebei area, among others.

In terms of functions, the NDRC is the heart of the BRI's strategic planning, responsible for leading and coordinating the work of various state agencies, state banks and SOEs and connecting domestic development initiatives with projects in neighbouring regions beyond China's borders as well as overseas. The NDRC is also involved in financial oversight and external debt control, as well as in international economic cooperation and dialogue between officials and experts. The NDRC's central role in the BRI's decision-making ecosystem is indicative of the core nature of the BRI as an ambitious project of economic development. Of course, in the Chinese authoritarian party-state, which is characterized by absence of separation of powers, the CCP has the unchecked capacity to interfere in the work of any state agency. However, the CCP also relies on the NDRC to safeguard the financial sustainability of proposed projects from planning to delivery. As such, the latter possess important administrative power in directing the BRI's development.

State-owned Asset Supervision and Administration Commission (SASAC)

SASAC was founded under the State Council in 2003 in an attempt to rationalize tasks that were previously spread around several sector-specific ministries. Like many features of the Chinese political system, the central SASAC is mirrored by province-level SASACs, which manage provincially controlled assets and are important BRI players in their own right. As the ultimate "owner" of all state-owned enterprises,

SASAC in 2018 managed assets worth $23 trillion, of which around $10 trillion are central SOE assets, while the remaining $13 trillion are provincial SOE assets (SASAC 2018). This makes SASAC the largest economic entity in the world but also "the most important organization in the world that nobody has heard of" (Naughton & Tsai 2015: 46). However, the sheer size of the organization does not correlate with its power within China's political ecosystem.

Rather than being an autonomous asset manager, SASAC was a way for the central state to delineate the border between the centrally managed economy and the private sector (see also the SOE entry below). SASAC was also designed to be a vehicle for corporate reform, but most of the top firms within SASAC (96 in 2020) have successfully resisted attempts at corporatization and continue to live as semi-governmental entities with limited transparency, protected markets and occasionally even full-blown monopolies.

Although SASAC was styled after Singapore's sovereign wealth fund Temasek, it has not yet shown any signs of being a vehicle for depoliticization of state assets. Because many SOEs are of ministerial rank, with some managers given full ministerial status, personnel issues are handled through the instrument of party cadre management rather than shareholder control. SASAC thus chooses neither the CEO nor the chairperson of the board of any of the SOEs under its control and its power to appoint executives exists only on paper (Naughton & Tsai 2015: 60). Lastly, despite being an "owner", SASAC does not collect all the revenue or dividends from the firms it nominally owns: most of the profits remain within each SOE group, while a share is turned over to the Ministry of Finance, which forwards most of it to SASAC, making it yet another interest group in China's convoluted state capitalist system (*ibid.*: 68).

State-owned enterprises (SOEs)

SOEs are a remnant of China's socialist economy, when all non-agricultural activity was controlled by some form of state enterprise or entity. Despite widespread privatization since 1978 – mainly through the "grasp the big, release the small" policy (*zhua da fang xiao* 抓大放小),

state ownership is not going away in China. The CCP continues to believe that state ownership provides income, enables control and offers governance tools – yet this result was not the end goal of an elaborate plan, but rather a consequence of a winding reform effort (Pearson 2015).

Initially, SOE reform focused on cutting costs for the state (which carried the costs of unprofitable enterprises), opening up non-strategic sectors to competition and attracting foreign investment and technology. While many lower-level SOEs were privatized (at least partly), this privatization was limited and affected the worst-performing assets, relieving the state of the obligation to pay the workers' wages. As Yasheng Huang notes, the Chinese state did exactly the opposite of what was expected in a transition from a planned socialist economy to private, free market economics (Huang 2008: 169). A collection of large and sometimes very valuable companies remained in the state's hands, while the chaff was sold off to the highest bidder.

A further distinguishing feature of Chinese SOEs is that, unlike the *chaebol* or *keiretsu* conglomerates of South Korea and Japan, each SOE group specializes only in one or two sectors (with some notable exceptions such as China Poly Group, an SOE linked to the PLA with interests in real estate, defence, fossil fuels and art auctioneering). SOEs are best imagined as vertical systems encompassing networked links with other corporate or government groups, what Lin and Milhaupt (2013) call "networked hierarchies". SOEs are also accountable to the state through contractual relations with relevant departments, and the revolving door of cadres serving in party, state and corporate positions enables "institutional bridging" (*ibid.*). On the other hand, while parent groups remain nominally owned by SASAC (see above), they exert a significant amount of fiscal autonomy, while the top personnel control is handled through the party's *nomenklatura* system of political appointments.

The SOEs of today thus represent the best assets that the state chose to retain under its control. Like other parts of China's political ecosystem, SOEs can be centrally managed (there are currently 96 national SOEs), or they can be owned by a provincial, city or township and county level government. While national SOEs work on the projects of the highest value, province-level SOEs make up a large proportion of projects, especially in developing countries. It has been estimated that most of the value of Chinese projects in Africa is in fact captured by provincial SOEs, who also exhibit different hiring practices, relying on local labour more often than national SOEs (Kernen & Lam 2014).

Most larger SOEs are organized as groups, where a core holding company owns the majority shareholdings in all functional subsidiaries. Because many SOEs were inefficient giants, a common solution was to spin off the most profitable and attractive parts of the parent company into "flagship" subsidiaries. Many of the Chinese companies traded on international stock markets are precisely such subsidiaries: Sinopec, listed in New York, Hong Kong and London, is, for example, the subsidiary of the China Petrochemical Corporation Group. This partial exposure to international markets allowed SOEs to raise significant amounts of capital, while also introducing an amount of market discipline into their listed operations. The companies active in the BRI are more often than not precisely such SOE spin-offs. Despite raising some capital through international markets, SOEs rely heavily on state-owned banks for their operations abroad. This organizational feature suggests access to capital for international investment or expansion is as much a function of political agility as it is of business acumen. The resulting set-up means Chinese SOEs face softer budget constraints than their counterparts in the west, but are in turn constrained in other, sometimes more opaque ways.

Provincial governments

China is often assumed to be a very centralized state, mainly due to its authoritarian political system that forbids open political competition to the CCP. This widely held view neglects the fact that, since Deng's reforms, subnational governments and provinces in particular, have emerged as a key engine of economic growth, a reality that has enhanced their policy autonomy (Montinola, Qian & Weingast 1995). Subnational governments are expected to follow the centre's directives but they enjoy considerable autonomy in terms of implementation, an arrangement that has been described as cooking on "separate stoves and a single menu" (Tsui & Wang 2004).

This autonomy extends to the realm of diplomacy, with provincial-level Foreign Affairs Offices performing a broad range of roles in advancing trade and business relations with foreign nations (Wong 2018; Duggan 2020). As a result, Chinese provinces have often spearheaded Beijing's economic and diplomatic initiatives. For example, the normalization of China's relations with South Korea in late 1980s to early 1990s, started with the provinces of Shandong, Liaoning and Jilin creating economic and institutional links with South Korea: establishing ferry links and special entry visas, sending and receiving delegations and facilitating trade and investment flows (Cheung & Tang 2001). Jilin, in particular, taking advantage of its Korean minority, pursued not only deeper trade relations but promoted regional cooperation that resulted in the Tumen River Area Development Programme between China, North Korea, Mongolia and Russia (Marton, McGee & Paterson 1995). This eventually developed into the Greater Tumen Initiative, an intergovernmental cooperation mechanism supported by the United Nations Development Programme.

Chinese provinces are involved in the BRI as political actors but also as financial stakeholders. Politically, provinces have attempted to influence the central government's decision-making on the BRI's development and direction, often competing with one another for Beijing's support and recognition. Their incentives are financial, in the form of acquiring funding for megaprojects such as roads, bridges and port infrastructure, but the political clout of being recognized as a key BRI province is also beneficial for provincial leaders. Zeng (2019: 211) explains the fierce competition between provinces to designate their cities as the starting point of the BRI, with Shaanxi (Xian) and Henan (Luoyang) competing for the land route and Fujian (Quanzhou), Jiangsu and Guangzhou (Beihai) competing for the origination point of the maritime route.

Moreover, the role of provincial-level SOEs in the development of the BRI is crucial. In Africa, for example, it has been noted that most Chinese SOEs are provincial-level, meaning that provinces, rather than Beijing, are involved in their decision-making and financing (Kernen & Lam 2014). In the context of China's decentralization, provincial governments rely on their SOEs to promote development and trade policies, while they retain decision-making power over the financing of projects valued between \$10 million and \$100 million (Duggan 2020). By simultaneously acting as gatekeepers of state financing for provincial-level SOEs and as stakeholders in their sound economic performance, provincial governments are influential, yet frequently overlooked actors in the development of the BRI. Their role demonstrates the BRI's nature as a framework for the coordination of goals, interests and resources within China's state capitalism ecosystem.

Chinese provinces deploy numerous strategies that are relevant to the shaping of the BRI and involve provincial-level SOEs and the provincial SASAC. Wong (2018) identifies three distinct strategies: trailblazing (where provinces take the initiative and persuade the centre to follow), carpetbagging (where provinces pay lip service to central policy but slowly subvert it to their needs) and resisting (where provinces ignore, delay or avoid implementing central policy). In the case of the BRI, this has led land-locked Henan province to, for example, innovate with an "Air Silk Road" to Luxembourg (Rabe & Kostka 2021), while Yunnan province has previously refused to close down the border with Myanmar despite being ordered to do so (Wong 2018: 752). Yunnan in particular has pursued an activist foreign policy that succeeded in incorporating the provincial diplomatic goals of positioning itself as a gateway to Southeast Asia within the broad envelope of the BRI as a central policy (Summers 2021). Similarly, neighbouring Guangxi province competed with Yunnan to become a vanguard of regional economic integration, for which it was rewarded with a specific mention in one of the BRI's foundational documents (Li 2019: 282). As provinces continue to drive innovation, shape and subvert central policy or even resist instructions from the top, they add to the complexity of the BRI despite certain limits on the scope and reach of their agency.

China's BRI banks

There are three types of banks active in financing BRI projects: China's first (and only) MDB, the AIIB, three so-called "policy banks", and state-owned commercial banks. The AIIB is the only bank that was created specifically with the BRI in mind, although ironically it is the bank that does the least lending to BRI projects. It also counts among its members countries such as India, which views the BRI with great suspicion yet chose to support (and draw on) the bank's funding mission. Since it was established in 2016, the bank has taken on a role of boosting China's influence in the global financial system instead of simply financing the BRI. The idea for a new multilateral bank focused on infrastructure grew out of a think tank led by a former vice-premier Zeng Peiyan in early 2013 and was eagerly accepted by China's leadership by the end of the year (Ren 2016: 437).

Although the AIIB shares many organizational aspects with western MDBs such as the World Bank, it differs in two main ways: its exclusive focus on infrastructure and its commitment to "non-interference" in domestic affairs. The latter was seen as a challenge to the conditionality of western MDBs and, by extension, to the Bretton Woods system of international finance. Despite the big waves the bank made at its inception, it remains a small player in BRI finance. Projected to lend $10–15 billion annually in its first six years, it had made only $10 billion of loans by 2019 and has been beset by a staff shortage (Tani 2019). The latest numbers available at the time of writing have the AIIB's total lending at $22 billion across 108 projects, of which just under $10 billion has been disbursed so far – a number that pales in comparison to BRI lending by China's state-owned policy banks.

The AIIB is important mainly because of its ability and willingness to work together with other MDBs, creating synergetic effects and transferring best practices on matters such as transparency, due diligence and compliance. As the Covid-19 pandemic hit the BRI, AIIB found a new role as the bank willing to provide short-term liquidity and investment into health systems. It is under this scheme that the bank lent $355 million to China and $750 million to India, among others (AIIB 2021: 36). The scheme also means the AIIB loosened its exclusive focus on physical infrastructure by supporting healthcare systems hit by the pandemic.

The vast majority of BRI financing originates from China's "policy banks": the CDB, China Exim and China Agricultural Development Bank. Policy banks are under direct control of the state and are used to drive forward state policy. The three policy banks were founded in 1994 in an effort to consolidate those financial operations that were directed by the state, separating them from the commercial state-owned banks such as the Industrial and Commercial Bank of China (ICBC).

Of the three, CDB and China Exim are relevant to the BRI. In the energy sector alone, the two banks have together disbursed $183 billion worth of loans across BRI (Global Development Center 2020) – dwarfing the contribution of the AIIB. Of the two, CDB is considered to be more market-oriented, but this was not always the case. When it was founded in 1994, the bank was seen as a pot of "free" money for SOEs and at one point had a catastrophic 32 per cent ratio of non-performing loans (Sanderson & Forsythe 2012: 60). Under the leadership of Chen Yuan, however, CDB not only became a profitable and trusted bank but began expanding its presence in the developing world. China Exim is, in contrast, an export credit agency dedicated to supporting the activities of China's businesses overseas. It does so by (1) providing letters of guarantee; (2) export credits to Chinese companies; (3) import credit to host states (on either commercial or concessional terms and backed by sovereign guarantees or assets); and (4) concessional foreign loans (Bräutigam & Gallagher 2014: 347).

Despite their dominant role as the bankers for the BRI, policy banks remain comparatively non-transparent. Even the source of their capital is unclear; although it is thought that China's dollar-denominated reserves form the bulk of the bank's capital, China Exim's "on-lending" (borrowing from other financial institutions to lend onwards) reached 46 per cent of its total outbound loans in 2006 (Klinger & Muldavin 2019: 11), suggesting China's policy banks have been well-integrated into global financial flows for years.

Large state-owned commercial banks have also been active in providing financing to Chinese investors or host-state entities along the BRI. The Bank of China (not to be confused with the People's Bank of China, the central bank of the PRC) has been present in Africa since 1997, for example, while the China Construction Bank set up shop there in 2000 (Bräutigam & Gallagher 2014). The largest of China's commercial banks, ICBC, became a major player by acquiring a 20 per cent stake in South Africa's Standard Bank – Africa's biggest lender by assets.

Lastly, other functional bureaucracies with active roles in the BRI include the MOFCOM and the Ministry of Foreign Affairs (MFA). Researchers have long noted the competition between different parts of the Chinese bureaucracy on foreign affairs (Gill & Reilly 2007; Jiang

2008; Liou 2009) and between MOFCOM and the MFA in particular (Jakobson & Knox 2010; Corkin 2011). Given that aid, trade and investment are all under the bureaucratic oversight of MOFCOM, it is not strange that the role of the MFA in the context of the BRI has been much smaller and confined to diplomatically supporting the various initiatives.

HIERARCHY AND LAYERING

On paper, the Chinese system appears very neatly structured. It is hierarchical, with the CCP paralleling and controlling state institutions and decision-making processes through a considerable degree of overlap between leading party and state positions. Although the CCP appears as omnipotent, the functional specialization of different organizations, bureaucracies and subnational actors creates vested interests that fuel internal competition, open up opportunities for individualistic and bureaucratic goals to shape the decision-making process, and sustain information gaps and risks associated with the lack of transparency and the weak rule of law. The BRI developed in this institutional context and therefore mirrors these basic characteristics.

Rather than the product of central design, the BRI has evolved gradually and in a manner that accommodates a multitude of commercial and political interests from subnational governments, SOEs, bureaucracies and banks, not to mention individual politicians and business people (Jones & Zou 2017; Zeng 2019; Summers 2020). Accordingly, the BRI has been described as a "loose policy envelope" (Jones & Zeng 2019), an "omnibus policy" (Summers 2016) and an "inherently decentralized endeavour" (Rogelja & Tsimonis 2020). These characterizations capture the BRI's fragmented and only loosely centralized pattern of implementation despite the very centralized fanfare and propaganda aiming at presenting it as China's – and personally Xi Jinping's – unique contribution to globalization. Interpretations that go beyond the "central masterplan" thesis and delve into the deep particularities and specifics of different cases of BRI-related investment, loan or institution building have unearthed an immensely rich and multilayered organization.

The multiplicity of interests, agendas, ambitions and actors that develop their agency under the BRI are impossible to fit in a single organizational diagram, let alone explain them as part of a categorical structure with orderly processes leading from A to Z. Hierarchies, of course, exist between the CCP and the state, among the different administrative levels, functional bureaucracies and SOEs and many decisions are taken and communicated in a top-down fashion. However, in addition to these hierarchies, the various political, financial and business actors operate within horizontal layers where they have to promote their interests vis-à-vis others. We distinguish four such layers: political, financial, international and local, each of which has unique conditions, formal or informal rules and actors. Chinese SOEs have to navigate in each one of these layers for their operations overseas to be successful.

Domestically, the *political layer* brings together Chinese party-state actors, including national and local leaders and governments, functional bureaucracies and state agencies. Despite the Chinese regime's enthusiastic endorsement of the BRI, obtaining state backing for a certain project requires extensive lobbying and negotiating by SOEs within a competitive environment where the interests of different sides need to be factored in their planning. After all, principal–agent problems lie at the heart of governance challenges in China as the CCP tries to keep state actors aligned to its policies and goals.

The *financial layer* involves Chinese investment and development agencies and banks. No doubt, if a project requires strong political support due to its strategic character, the funds will be made available eventually. But for most ventures, securing financial support from the state is far from straightforward, as there is significant competition among SOEs. The financial layer involves formal processes (applications, business plans, tendering procedures, export credits, project insurance), but also informal practices (clientelism, *guanxi*) that undermine due diligence in financial decisions.

In the *international layer* Chinese SOEs have to identify investment opportunities, attract international financing, comply with international standards and foreign direct investment (FDI) screening mechanisms, and deal with (often negative) perceptions regarding their role as instruments of neocolonialism or agents of a malign authoritarian regime. "Going global" means that SOEs have to abandon the "comfort zone" of state paternalism, exposing them to the economic and political pitfalls of global capitalism, but this risk is mitigated by the support of banks and carefully managed competition. The BRI is a platform that enables SOEs to partially address their growth challenges with the state's financial and diplomatic support, but once we move away from the domestic context, risk nevertheless increases considerably and there is a limit to what the Chinese state can do to help. What is more, part of SOEs internationalization is "going local".

The *host country layer* is the stage where Chinese SOEs become embedded in the local context of their investment. In this layer, SOEs may enjoy diplomatic backing by the Chinese state but, in most cases, they are largely on their own when dealing with local political, business and societal actors. As a result they often risk becoming entangled in local controversies and political rivalries, as well as in clientelist exchanges and networks of corruption, which may damage their corporate image and harm the sustainability of their ventures. Chinese scholars have criticized poor planning in this regard, even comparing the BRI with the Great Leap Forward, noting that projects fail because of informational asymmetries in local contexts that Chinese business actors are not aware of (Zhai 2015: 55). This layer is also crucial to understand the role of the BRI in the heating up of a global competition with the USA, where small states can sometimes profit by pursuing hedging strategies between the two giants (Schindler, DiCarlo & Paudel 2021: 5), demonstrating how we understand these layers to be in a constant interaction with each other.

SOEs must skilfully address the challenges present in all these layers. For instance, a provincial-level SOE needs the backing of the local (or even national level) CCP leadership at the political layer; has to convince state agencies and banks for the sustainability of its intended investment at the financial layer; has to compete with other profit-seeking companies and strong business interests at the international layer; and as a newcomer investor has to negotiate with the foreign governments, businesses and communities at the host country layer. The sum of pressures, limitations and opportunities present at each layer and the ability of SOEs to balance them in their favour, determine the success or failure of individual projects, which ultimately determines the success or failure of the BRI as a whole.

A decline of opportunities for financing due to an economic crisis or the accumulation of non-performing debts, the loss of political support for lavish spending abroad, rising hostility to Chinese investors in many countries, or extensive local entanglement that makes a project unsustainable can all have a negative effect on specific projects and on the entire BRI. For instance, the $87 billion CPEC has attracted a lot of attention in terms of its profitability and sustainability. With significant delays in delivering the envisaged projects, empty ports, airports and special economic zones, and the risk of deteriorating Pakistan's ability to repay its debt, voices questioning its overambitious planning have emerged on both sides (Anderlini, Sender & Bokhalri 2018). A recent inquiry by a Pakistani government committee found that several Chinese companies inflated their costs – hardly a win-win situation (Haqqani 2020).

In the distant Czech Republic, a private Chinese investment company, CEFC China Energy, and its head, Ye Jianming, emerged as the key broker of a broad range of deals between the two countries, boasting a close relationship with Czech president Zeman. However, it soon emerged that CEFC was involved in shady deals and corruption cases and failed to fulfil its financial commitments. Despite being a private company, CEFC seriously damaged Sino-Czech relations, casting doubt on future economic cooperation (Garlick 2019).

In Kenya, meanwhile, a $2 billion project to build a coal power plant near the UNESCO world heritage town of Lamu was cancelled after the country's court annulled the project's environmental permit, citing the developer's failure to consult the local community. Although spearheaded by a Sino-Kenyan joint venture and backed by an ICBC financing package, the developer did not accurately read the growing anti-coal sentiment in the country, ultimately being stopped by a legal challenge from civil society groups (Waruru 2019).

The BRI is organized along vertical hierarchies that coexist with horizontal layers, meaning political and business actors are exposed to different pressures and dilemmas. In particular, the further we move from the political and financial layers, the trickier it becomes for the Chinese state to influence developments on the ground. This difficulty involves both traditional principal–agent dilemmas in relation to the conduct of Chinese SOEs and individual businesses, but also the many traps and dangers present when operating in foreign socioeconomic and political contexts with limited knowledge of local dynamics, which has often led to failed investments. For Chinese SOEs, this complexity is even higher as each layer requires skilful negotiation and quick adaptation to the conditions present, be that successfully lobbying officials for the necessity of a project, competing for state financing with other SOEs, navigating through the "terra incognita" of launching a venture in a new country, and the risks that arise when inevitably getting embedded into local economic, political, social and clientelist networks.

DIFFERENT THINGS TO DIFFERENT PEOPLE

In the previous pages we discussed the BRI's ecosystem and origins, its most important players and the complex ways they relate to one another. There are three key takeaways from this chapter. First, the BRI has to be understood as an extension of China's state capitalist ecosystem. In practice this means that its development simultaneously reflects the centre's preoccupation with economic security and the interests of its key actors, including individual Chinese leaders, local governments, functional bureaucracies and SOEs. This plurality of interests and agendas drives the BRI's expansion and the evolution of its character equally to the strategic planning of Beijing, if not more.

Second, as nothing comes from nothing, we can trace the BRI to similar projects of domestic regional economic development and integration. We dare to say that even if the BRI did not exist as a name, it could well exist as a reality given the plethora of China-centred development and cooperation initiatives, forums and institutions that have sprung up since the 2000s. The fact that Xi Jinping decided to introduce the BRI platform to integrate all these initiatives shows an evolving strategic thinking but is also a recognition of the many challenges involved for SOEs and the need to address the omnipotent principal–agent problems that permeate the central government's relations with state entities.

And third, we can ill afford simplistic narratives of the BRI that present it as a singular design that is centrally executed. China's rise fuels the burgeoning economic activity of the BRI and indeed the centre's strategic interests are present, but at the same time we must not forget that its dynamism is also business-driven. Ye (2021) calls this "fragmented motives and policies", pointing out that different parts of the Chinese party-state want different things from the BRI. While the political elites around Xi employed a geopolitical language, the bureaucracy was unable to translate this into a coherent and comprehensive policy, leading to a situation where state economic actors (mainly SOEs, but also policy banks) have shaped the implementation of the situation on the ground (*ibid.*: 201).

Our view aligns very closely with Ye in trying to understand the complexity and many feedback mechanisms involved in the Initiative. While Ye focuses mainly on the domestic Chinese political context, our accounts also include various host-state actors as important stakeholders that affect how "China's globalization" plays out on the ground. The BRI is therefore undoubtedly "political", but many simpler accounts of the BRI overemphasize geopolitical aspects at the expense of analytical precision and creating a zero-sum interpretation of Chinese economic activities abroad. In the next chapter, we will take on the task of addressing the difficult question of "what is political about the BRI" and unpack the relationship between Chinese politics and business as it unfolds across the world.

3

Is it China's grand strategy?

Since the 1990s, researchers, commentators and politicians have been asking the question "What does China want?" What are China's ambitions and goals, given its dramatic ascendance as an economic superpower? And is its "peaceful rise" possible? (Segal 1999; Johnston 2003; Buzan 2010; Brown 2017). Following the collapse of the USSR, the first version of the "China Threat scenario" emerged among US conservative policy circles, but China's increasing openness after Tiananmen, culminating in its 2001 entry into the WTO, rendered it irrelevant until the end of the Hu-Wen era.

The 2010s, however, witnessed an increasing alarmism about the rapidly expanding presence of Chinese economic actors globally. When US anxiety focused mainly on the military and political rise of China, its seemingly capitalist economy had provided a much-needed tonic to calm the nerves. But now a more robust rearticulation of the China Threat idea stated that Chinese activities in the economic field also hide malicious intentions. Under this prism, the BRI is seen as the economic pillar of Xi Jinping's grand strategy to reshape the global balance of power to China's favour. The group supporting this view could not be more diverse, including voices from the left, centre, right and far-right of the political spectrum.

Is the BRI really a strategy, perhaps even a "grand" one? Can it reveal to us China's plans and intentions? We will confront this question by starting from the notion of "grand strategy" itself. The study of "grand strategy" can help analyze a country's intentions by taking a step back and getting a more holistic perspective on whether a unified picture exists or not, thereby linking together different pieces of the puzzle. However, the idea of a grand strategy can also act as a lens that distorts reality to provide justification for a certain policy preference. Think, for instance, about the Cold War era "domino theory", which assumed that the USSR's grand strategy was to export revolution to different parts of the world and set up puppet regimes controlled by Moscow. This assumption distorted the nature of anticolonial struggles in places such as Vietnam and provided the rationale for the US military intervention. So, searching for a grand strategy can help us identify it, as well as deliberately or unintentionally invent it!

Grand strategy guides state action by linking means to national goals. The concept, famously articulated by Clausewitz, refers to the mobilization of a wide range of diplomatic, economic, social, bureaucratic, military and other means at the state's disposal to pursue its goals peacefully and/or on the battleground. International relations historians and theorists have long debated how and why a grand strategy is formed, emphasizing the international environment and the security threats and opportunities it creates for states, or alternatively the impact of domestic politics, the agendas of different actors and the material limitations and constraints present (Kennedy 1991; Strachan 2005; Brands 2014). Most examinations of grand strategy, however, combine these two perspectives, recognizing that both international and domestic dynamics are at play in its formation, implementation, success or failure. Going back to the example of US grand strategy during the Cold War, authors have recognized the threats, tensions and dilemmas present in the international system but also the impact of domestic actors, such as the military-intelligence establishment and the role of different presidents in the course of superpower antagonism.

More interestingly, a different approach to the study of grand strategy has turned on the concept itself, and especially on its somewhat mechanistic assumption on the link between means and goals (Mitzen 2015). In an idealized world, states are rational actors that maximize the utility and efficiency of their means in pursuing clear goals. In the real world, however, big gaps exist between how a grand strategy is imagined and how it is implemented, how different domestic elite and bureaucratic actors prioritize different goals and means, while information gaps and misperceptions undermine any notion of an "objective" international environment with a straightforward impact on policy (Betts 2000).

What is more, historical and cultural factors, the characteristics of political regimes and the domestic insecurities of rulers, are variables that may translate to policy choices that do not conform to what an external observer would expect. The comparison between Meiji Japan and Qing China is very telling in this regard. Faced with the same threat of western imperialism in the 1800s, Japan chose a path towards rapid modernization, while the cultural superiority of the Sinocentric worldview of the Qing, coupled with institutional weaknesses, undermined their ability to understand and respond to a rapidly changing international environment (Fairbank 1942).

The existence of different variables and trajectories in the formation and implementation of a grand strategy inevitably translates into complexity for both policymakers and analysts. To make matters worse, as the BRI is an ongoing economic endeavour that lacks a clear military-security dimension, most of the arguments that designate it as a grand strategy are non-falsifiable along this line of reasoning: "if the BRI does not look like a military strategy, it is because it is so well-camouflaged, and therefore even more threatening".

In this chapter, we will discuss some of the most popular relevant depictions of the BRI as (1) China's equivalent to the Monroe Doctrine and the Marshall Plan designed to challenge US hegemony; (2) a military-logistical complex intended to project Chinese power across the globe; (3) an attempt to restructure the regional (in Asia) and global order with new ideas, norms and institutions; and (4) a "silent invasion" against democracies. We will identify problems with all these propositions by analyzing the BRI's key flagship projects, corridors and nodes, focusing on deciphering its geopolitical logic. Key components of the BRI serve China's domestic and economic security, and investments in infrastructure by SOEs and private companies create interests that can "pull" the attention of Chinese diplomacy to specific countries.

However, the BRI is far from a grand strategy. It appears much more like a platform that serves multiple economic (engaging spare industrial capacity, intensifying trade, offshoring dirty industries, investing dollars at higher returns than in the domestic or US Treasury bonds) and security goals (diversifying energy supply, shoring up allies, preventing cross-border insurgencies). Moreover, the BRI accommodates the bottom-up initiative of business actors by design, making it a rather ingenious way to leverage China's advantages, while keeping SOEs busy. As Min Ye succinctly called it, it is "state-mobilized globalization" (Ye 2020). But this proliferation of actors and moving parts also means it is a fluid effort without a predetermined goal, rather than an all-out mobilization of the Chinese state's military, diplomatic and material resources.

A NEW MONROE DOCTRINE AND A MARSHALL PLAN 2.0?

If the BRI is (part of) a grand strategy aimed at displacing American hegemony, how does it compare to the rise of the USA? The BRI is sometimes compared to the Monroe Doctrine, due to its assumed hegemonic and exclusionary nature (Carpio 2021; Nugent & Campell 2021; Zolinger Fujii 2021, to name but a few representative examples). Alternatively, the BRI has been interpreted as a Chinese version of the Marshall Plan, because of its emphasis on economic development (Shen 2016; Beeson 2018). We consider both comparisons to be far-fetched. However, given how often they are invoked in public discourse, we will begin unpacking the idea of the BRI as a grand strategy by looking at these comparisons more closely.

The Monroe Doctrine of 1823 has been characterized as a "hands-off" declaration, a "keep out" sign put up by the USA to exclude European colonial powers from the western hemisphere (Jackson 2016: 65). When it was introduced, the Monroe Doctrine did not reflect the military power of the USA, so it was not taken seriously by the great powers of the day. The USA was in this sense a minor revisionist power challenging the dominant norms of the time (Zolinger Fujii 2021). The USA first invoked it in 1865, against French intervention in Mexico (Sexton 2011: 293–5), and again in the early 1900s, but it was after the First World War that it came to be globally recognized and respected.

The Doctrine evolved from being a non-interventionist call to establishing the "right" of the USA to intervene in the domestic affairs of American states, thereby rendering the North and South American continents a zone of exclusive political influence for the USA (*ibid.*: 438). The success of the Doctrine is seen as the beginning of the emergence of the USA as a global power. Analytically, the Doctrine is used as a "blueprint" for the study of other aspiring superpowers. In this view, securing supremacy and excluding other rivals from a certain region is the necessary first step before advancing to global projection of power. The German *Lebensraum* and the Japanese *Dai Tōa Kyōeiken* (Greater East Asia Co-Prosperity Sphere) are other well-known attempts to rise to global power status by first establishing regional hegemony. Hawkish US analysts have even accused China of "copying" Japan's hegemonic plan in an effort to "exact revenge on its neighbours" that apparently shows "classic examples of historical rage" (Mendis & Wang 2020).

Many China Threat theories build on the idea that history repeats itself. This is why many analysts believe China's rise will follow the same path to superpower status that inevitably starts with establishing a regional hegemony. Predictions about a "Chinese Monroe Doctrine" go back to at least the late 1990s, when the China Threat scenario first emerged. As the pre-eminent American realist scholar John Mearsheimer noted in his treatise on the *Tragedy of Great Power Politics*: "We would also expect China to develop its own version of the Monroe Doctrine, directed at the United States. Just as the United States made it clear to distant great powers that they were not allowed to meddle in the western hemisphere, China will make it clear that American interference in Asia is unacceptable" (2001: 415).

Perhaps not surprisingly, in search of evidence of China's attempt to exert hegemony over a region, the BRI has been interpreted as an attempt to *exclude* the economic, and eventually the political and security, influence of the USA from China's periphery (Maçães 2018: 136). The argument is compelling, in effect depicting China as luring central Asian and Southeast Asian states with investments and tying them to Chinese interests through joint projects and "debt traps". Eventually, the argument continues, economic dependence will spill over into geopolitics, gradually eroding US influence and weakening its security architecture in East Asia.

China's insistence that the BRI does not exclude any power from joining, repeatedly emphasizing its inclusive character, is brushed aside as insincere. Little mention is made of the USA's own wavering commitment to Asia-Pacific integration, as illustrated by its withdrawal from the Trans-Pacific Partnership under the Trump administration and continued frostiness towards the initiative under President Biden.

Furthermore, the fact that BRI countries continue to engage with multiple trade partners and initiatives in their effort to maximize economic gains through a hedging strategy (as shown by Schindler, DiCarlo & Paudel 2021: 5) is overlooked, presumably because it does not fit the narrative on dependency.

This comparison between the Monroe Doctrine and the BRI largely makes sense because it fits the simple realist model of hegemony that continues to dominate influential parts of the international relations discipline. The trouble with simple models is that we sometimes start to look for proof of their predictions. This is not to say that the BRI is not exclusionary, but rather that in its present form it does not act as a hegemonic policy aimed at excluding the USA and its allies from Asian affairs. For the BRI to truly become an attempt to exclude non-Asian powers from its region, it will be of utmost importance to study how Japan positions itself. So far, competition between the two Asian giants has taken place precisely in the area of infrastructure bids in Southeast Asia (Pavlićević & Kratz 2017), but neither side has attempted to "exclude" the other through political pressure on host states, and both parties recently acceded to a regional trade agreement that also includes Australia and New Zealand, the Regional Comprehensive Economic Partnership. If the BRI is meant to exclude the West from the region, it has not succeeded so far. If anything, it has galvanized the staunchest US allies in East Asia to up its game.

Another long-standing comparison that analysts often employ to make sense of the BRI is the Marshall Plan, both in flattering terms (Feng & Liang 2019) and as a point of contrast (Narins & Agnew 2020). Implemented between 1948 and 1951, the European Recovery Program, as it was officially called, provided approximately $12 billion of aid and $1 billion in loans to western European countries to promote their economic reconstruction following the devastation of the Second World War (Hogan 1987: 414–15). The Marshall Plan was an effort by the USA to speed up the economic recovery of allied nations in order to curb the rising influence of communist movements. The Plan was the first step in building the security and economic architecture of western Europe, with NATO (established in 1949) providing military deterrence and the European Economic Community (established in 1957) and the OECD, first established in 1948 as the Organisation for European Economic

Co-operation (OEEC), setting the foundations for economic growth and regional integration.

The comparison with the Marshall Plan highlights the BRI's scale and emphasis on creating growth multipliers. Estimated at around $130 billion in 2020 value, the Plan subsidized imports of fuel and raw materials, fertilizers and seeds, semi-manufactured products and machinery, all of which contributed to accelerating economic reconstruction. Between 1948 and 1951, industrial production in Europe increased by 43 per cent as a direct result of American aid (Hogan 1987: 415). The BRI, announced five years after the 2008 financial crisis, envisages $1 trillion will be spent by 2030 (OECD 2018: 3), mainly on large-scale infrastructure projects that will facilitate connectivity and promote trade (Shen 2019). The BRI is in some sense larger in scope, but it is nowhere near as generous because China's money will for the most part be repaid, with interest.

In both cases, institutionalization became an important feature. The USA and China set up agencies and international organizations to coordinate the distribution of funds and maximize efficiency. In the case of the Marshall Plan, the two key institutions were the Economic Cooperation Administration, managed by the USA, and the OEEC, run by European countries to combine their efforts in reconstruction and development. The OEEC was superseded by the OECD in 1961, which is still the most important institutional legacy of the Plan. In the case of the BRI, as detailed in Chapter 1, we have witnessed a proliferation of multilateral forums, cooperation mechanisms and funding institutions, such as the Silk Road Fund, the AIIB and regional forums such as the China-CEEC, among many others.

Lastly, both the Marshall Plan and the BRI mirror the characteristics of the domestic model of development of their countries of origin, with the first promoting trade liberalization against the economic nationalism and protectionism of the 1920s and 1930s (Hogan 1987), and the second being driven by Chinese SOEs and agreements between states, rather than private business entities. However, the similarities between the Marshall Plan and the BRI stop here.

The Marshall Plan was a time-limited financial stimulus programme, composed almost entirely of aid to subsidize imports and promote free trade, and accompanied by a rapidly evolving, highly militarized collective security architecture. The Plan reflected the rising Cold War mentality that became hegemonic over the next four decades, interpreting all political developments from the prism of a zero-sum game: a loss for the USA was a gain for the USSR and vice versa. As such, it was exclusionary and security-oriented by nature. On the other hand, the BRI is open-ended, consists primarily of loans by Chinese development banks (mainly China Exim and CDB), is directed at large infrastructure projects and has no clear security component. BRI projects have gone ahead in a variety of political regimes, from democracies to autocracies. Institutionalization is still "shy" and horizontal, consisting of weak financial commitments and limited to economic affairs. From its outset, the Marshall Plan became the basis of extensive cooperation and contributed to the idea of an integrated, democratic, liberal West, yet the BRI carries no such ambitions for regional integration, other than the occasional reference to "win-win" cooperation.

Furthermore, the Marshall Plan's projected model of development, which promoted a consumption-based global economy (Shen & Chan 2018: 3), came to challenge the economic nationalism of the interwar period and Soviet communism. The Marshall Plan was profoundly incompatible with any notion of protectionism and a centrally planned economy. The BRI, on the other hand, despite originating from China's experience with state-led capitalism since the early 1980s, does not need to replace one economic model with another.

From the viewpoint of western economic liberalism, one can identify many problems with China's model, especially when the authoritarian nature of its state is factored in. However, China had already become a centrepiece of global capitalist networks of production long before it announced the BRI (Freymann 2020). As we will argue in the following chapters, the conduct of its SOEs raises issues of fair competition, compliance and sustainability, but the existence of SOE investing in infrastructure and promoting trade does not require a challenge to the liberal economic order. China's idiosyncratic brand of state capitalism questions many liberal assumptions about the role of the state but does not sit too far from the developmental models of Japan, South Korea or Taiwan. Ultimately, the BRI can be compatible with global capitalism and it is hardly a compelling alternative model that could replace or overthrow it.

Zhou Fangyin, a leading Chinese analyst of the BRI, lucidly argues that any economic goals of the BRI might face significant obstacles because of security considerations, especially if the BRI inadvertently triggers "strategic games" between global powers (Zhou 2015: 66). Given the BRI's reach into the "back yards" of several great powers, it seems unlikely it will manage to create an exclusive zone of interest without antagonizing a long list of China's friends and foes. For this reason, Chinese scholars have argued against the creation of blocs and alliances that may divert the developmental orientation of the BRI and have urged the government to enhance transparency and pursue cooperation with small and major powers alike, including the USA (Zhao 2018; Gao 2019).

From the above discussion, it becomes evident that any similarities between the BRI and the Monroe Doctrine or the Marshall Plan are coincidental. Even if China has set out to create an exclusive sphere of influence, replace the global economic order or lure countries into collective security agreements against a rival superpower, the BRI has not delivered on these imagined goals. Having said that, it would be naive to uncritically accept China's stated goals as simply promoting the Silk Road spirit of "peace and cooperation, openness and inclusiveness, mutual learning and mutual benefit" (Xi 2017). Decoupling geo-economic designs from geopolitical and security considerations is analytically ill-advised and China's silence over these aspects creates ample space for speculation. After all, the BRI's strategic goals might be vague but they are not indiscernible. In case after case, Chinese loans and infrastructural spending have benefited Chinese actors above all others and have often been used to shore up autocratic or corrupt regimes in host countries. Moreover, even if the BRI is not a "grand strategy" like the Marshall Plan, China's expanding economic interests may yet require it to set up a more ambitious security policy. But is the BRI it, or will it ironically frustrate China's presumed hegemonic ambitions?

A HEGEMONIC PROJECT?

On 22 February 2011, China began evacuating its citizens from war-torn Libya in an operation that involved the PLA navy and air force. The "Great Evacuation", as the Chinese media called it, extracted over 35,000

Chinese nationals from the country (Shesterinina 2016: 823). The evacuation marks the first time China has directly intervened in a conflict zone to extract its nationals without the explicit permission of the host government, or a clear UN Security Council mandate. It also illustrates, in graphic terms, the risks that China's increased activity overseas brings to its citizens and property. Much like Britain or the USA, the argument goes, China too will have to develop a globe-spanning security infrastructure to support its economic ambitions. And since prevention is better than cure, why stop there? Why not deploy permanent military bases around the world, intervene in internal affairs of other states, or better yet, have allied states follow your lead? Hegemony, unlike domination, is a cost-effective strategy. But is the BRI it? And if the BRI is a hegemonic strategy, where can we locate its military component?

To answer these questions, we should determine how and when security aspects shape decisions on the BRI's formation and direction. There are two ways to formulate this question: either the BRI exists to promote an existing security agenda — let us call it a hegemonic ambition — or it will change China's future foreign security calculus and create a hegemony by necessity. We can find evidence to support either statement. The first sets out to show how the BRI could erase the boundary between China's domestic and international security concerns, in effect expanding the CCP's domestic will to power beyond China's borders. The second, meanwhile, is a historical analogy with Britain and the USA, both of which found military might to be necessary for the maintenance of an economic empire. As National Bureau of Asian Research analyst Nadège Rolland puts it: "China's Ministry of National Defense publicly denies that BRI has any military or geostrategic intent. Even if that is truly the case, the priority Beijing has given to BRI for the last six years has created an overall acceleration and geographic expansion of Chinese overseas activities that will inevitably generate the need for some level of state and military protection" (Rolland 2019a: 2).

But will this need result in a creation of a Chinese regional hegemony, as Mearsheimer would expect? Rolland's argument is compelling but it is hard to disprove. Let us therefore first turn to the links between China's domestic and international security concerns with a simple question: does the BRI articulate an ambition to set up a military hegemony beyond China's borders? The BRI has three predecessor policies with strong security dimensions to them, which are in turn linked to key national security priorities for Beijing: the GWD strategy in Xinjiang, the CPEC, and China's effort to neutralize the Malacca dilemma and secure/diversify China's sea lines of communication, all of which we examine in turn by appraising them against the idea of hegemony (be it one born out of ambition or necessity).

The GWD strategy and the BRI cross China's most rebellious area, the Xinjiang Uyghur Autonomous Region, as it is officially known. Xinjiang was cut off from its natural hinterland in Central Asia during Cold War hostilities between China and the Soviet Union, but as Soviet successor states sprang up in the region, new security concerns replaced the fear of all-out Soviet invasion. Cross-border support for Uyghur separatism still ranks as the number one security challenge for China, but the BRI intersects with this concern in somewhat unexpected ways. True to its developmental ideas, the CCP had hoped that developing the region economically would pacify the Uyghurs (Hopper & Webber 2009), but evidence suggests modernization has perpetuated and even complicated ethnic tensions (Clarke 2007).

The BRI, with its international dimension, thus presents two challenges. First, China must ensure cross-border connectivity does not result in increased traffic of weapons or other sources of support for Uyghur fighters. On the other hand, the railroads, roads and pipelines now linking China to its western neighbours needed to be protected and the only way to do this – given Russia's strategic entitlement in Central Asia – was through a multilateral security effort that involved Moscow. Thus, the Shanghai Cooperation Organization (SCO) was born. As predicted by Rolland, increased economic activities did correlate with an increased security involvement, but this took the form of engaging regional actors in joint "counterterrorism" efforts, selling them military equipment and pressuring them to sign bilateral extradition agreements (Pantucci 2019).

Very few of the SCO's activities relate directly to the BRI, yet it is easy to link them to China's domestic security fears. The SCO, rather than protecting BRI infrastructure and personnel, seems to fit domestic counterinsurgency efforts in its member states and is hardly a vision of a China-centred alliance. As the SCO expanded to include Pakistan, India and Iran, it became an even less likely vehicle for a Chinese grand strategy in the region. If anything, the SCO exists to bolster a sovereigntist understanding of security, creating a club of governments worried about non-state actors. That there is some correlation and geographical overlap between the SCO and BRI does not imply causation: China will continue to rely on bilateral security arrangements wherever possible, with domestic security as the prime motivator. As such, the BRI has not significantly altered Central Asia's security architecture.

The BRI may not be about creating a regional hegemony in Central Asia but it does clearly figure in China's security calculus. Pakistan, on the other hand, is China's oldest friend and the closest thing Beijing has to an ally. This makes it the best-case study to show how China's thinking on regional security intersects with the BRI. Arguably the most intensive corridor of the BRI globally, the CPEC runs from Xinjiang to the port of Gwadar on the Arabian Sea, crossing not only fierce terrain, but some of Pakistan's most unruly regions such as Balochistan. Not surprisingly, Chinese assets and citizens have been attacked several times over the past decades, particularly by the Balochistan Liberation Army. As if regional insurgencies were not enough, Imran Khan's election victory in 2018 initially stalled many CPEC projects amid concerns of inflated costs and internal tussles about which province gets which project. It was not until the Pakistani army took an interest in CPEC that the project was re-energized in early 2020 (Rehman & Walker 2020).

Much like in Central Asia, Sino-Pakistani security cooperation predates the BRI and centres around counterinsurgency, arms sales and joint military technology development. A lot of attention has been directed towards Gwadar port, which could shorten China's oil supply route to the Gulf, yet the technical and economic feasibility of a pipeline across the 4,693-metre-high Khunjerab pass in the Karakoram mountains is highly doubtful (Erickson & Collins 2010). Alternatively, the port could serve as a useful service station for the Chinese navy and rumours have circulated about a potential Chinese base being built in Jiwani, just west of Gwadar (Rajagopalan 2018). For the moment, however, the only military task force based in the port is Pakistan's Task Force 88, and the port serves Pakistan's strategic goals much better than anyone else's.

Yet hegemony is about more than just stationing troops or signing military alliances. Could China instrumentalize the economic focus of the BRI to expand its hard power in Pakistan? It is often suggested that China has leverage over Pakistan because of the debt Pakistan has incurred. Indeed, Pakistan has taken out $28 billion in loans from China (government, state-owned bank and AIIB credit) between 2010 and 2019. This represents more than a third of the grand total of $74 billion of loans and credits contracted in the same period (Government of Pakistan 2019). The adage applies here: if you owe the bank a hundred dollars, that is your problem, but if you owe the bank a hundred million (or 28 billion), that is the bank's problem. Pakistan is currently renegotiating around $17 billion of the bilateral debt owed to China through the Debt Service Suspension Initiative. Judging by China's record, the loans will likely be deferred in a protracted and opaque process, rather than written off or swapped for equity (Kratz, Mingey & D'Alelio 2020).

Despite the increase in non-performing loans, the churn of BRI loans has fed Chinese SOEs, recycled China's dollar reserves and catered both to Beijing's and to local political priorities. At best, China will benefit from closer ties with Pakistan, strengthen its SOEs and gain a friendly port in the Arabian Sea. At worst, it will become over-exposed in a volatile country, entangling itself in internal power struggles that decrease rather than increase China's security.

And what of the maritime part of the BRI? One geostrategic theory commonly associated with it is the idea that China is putting together a "string of pearls", stretching from the South China Sea, past the Strait of Malacca and all the way to the Suez Canal – although even the port of Piraeus makes an appearance in some think tank reports on the subject (Pelagidis 2019). The term "string of pearls" first appeared on the think tank circuit in the 2000s but gained traction once Xi Jinping announced the Maritime Silk Road in 2014 as a complementary strategy to the land "belt" he first mentioned in late 2013. Ironically, the unified policy slogan made it possible for hawkish observers to label an incongruous collection of ports, bridges, cargo terminals, military bases and airports as a lucid geostrategic plan aimed at ensuring naval domination in the South China Sea and Indian Ocean. The precise list of pearls is a matter of debate, but the Kyaukpyu port on Myanmar, Chittagong in Bangladesh, Hanbantota in Sri Lanka, the Maldives, Gwadar port in Pakistan, Bagamoyo port in Tanzania and the Chinese naval base in Djibouti are most frequently associated with the idea. Some military analysts have even included Hainan Province, as well as the disputed reefs of the South China Sea where China has been aggressively developing military installations (Pehrson 2006: 3).

As with China's interests in Central Asia, domestic security priorities determine foreign strategies. The expansion of military facilities in the South China Sea is not entirely outside the norm of China's maximalist territorial claims. But how do we ascertain whether China's naval ambitions beyond the South China Sea, as expressed in the Maritime Silk Road, are aimed at creating a hegemonic position in the Indian Ocean? One way is to look beyond China's immediate and claimed area, where a degree of militarization is to be expected. Are China's pearls a necklace choking India and thwarting US naval power, or are they something else?

PRAGMATIC RESPONSES TO GEOPOLITICAL DILEMMAS

Let us begin with the one "pearl" in the Indian Ocean that is undoubtedly a military facility. In 2017 China opened its first permanent overseas naval base in Djibouti. So far the base has been used mainly to support China's peacekeeping and anti-piracy operations (the latter ran in parallel to, rather than part of, the international anti-piracy effort). It is not a stretch to imagine anti-piracy and peacekeeping as a convenient cover under which China is advancing its geostrategic goals. Djibouti is a country that lacks many resources but a strategic position is not one of them. Unsurprisingly, it is a desirable destination for foreign militaries and hosts the Chinese, US, French, Japanese, Spanish, Saudi and Italian militaries. This makes for an interesting paradox: China's base in Djibouti is not at all unusual in the international sense but it is "norm-breaking" in the domestic sense (Rolland 2019a). This suggests that we cannot rely on China always following its own red lines on foreign military bases and is the clearest sign yet (along with the construction of an aircraft carrier fleet) that Beijing does indeed have naval ambitions that go well beyond the South China Sea. But the question we are trying to answer here is not speculation about China's future military plans. Rather, we are trying to ascertain whether the BRI will significantly expand or aid such plans. Ports are often mentioned in this regard because of their assumed "double" use as both civilian and military infrastructure.

Not all BRI ports serve the same function though. Brewster (2017) divides them into three types: service ports that facilitate local trade (such as Chittagong), trans-shipment hubs that serve larger regions (Hambantota) and gateway ports that are terminals for new overland link to China (Gwadar and Kyaukpyu). Brewster maintains it is the new gateway ports that most significantly alter the strategic balance of the Indian Ocean, but not in a way that is immediately obvious. These ports and their associated overland connectivity installations (roads, rails, pipelines) are not great at supporting Chinese naval power projection. Military assets require a higher standard of construction; for example, for roll-on/roll-off of heavy-tracked vehicles, as well as deeper berths, special cold storage chains for blood and other organic materials of war – something that Chinese and US analysts agree is a very difficult undertaking that would require a great amount of civilian–military cooperation (Kardon 2020).

While recent legislation on military–civilian fusion (*junmin ronghe* 军民融合) goes a long way to ensure the interoperability of civilian assets for military use in times of crisis or war, access to foreign ports does not depend just on the technical specifications of the port, but must also account for the sovereign rights of host states. All the host countries have asserted their sovereign right over allowing military vessels to berth in their ports, meaning any permanent facilities would be subject to political negotiation. Moreover, most of the ports are fairly exposed and would not significantly challenge Indian naval power. Instead, what the gateway ports and the new overland connections to China do is further entangle Beijing into the affairs of states around the Indian Ocean.

In the past, geography afforded China "... the luxury of being able to avoid getting its hands dirty in these politically unstable countries" (Brewster 2017: 285). But once pipelines and roads more firmly connected China to its neighbours, the need to work with an array of regimes and governments replaced the high-minded aloofness of years gone by. In Pakistan, Myanmar, Sri Lanka and the Maldives, domestic political shifts have strained China's much- vaunted "non-interference" policies, although not always in a way that would be conducive to a Chinese hegemonic expansion.

China's approach to politics in the Persian Gulf is a good example of how the BRI interacts with the region's power dynamics. The Gulf is where China's geo-economic interests (a stable supply of oil and sea lanes of communication) exist in a precarious regional order riven by Saudi–Iranian competition and US military dominance. In some ways, Iran makes for a natural ally in the region. Like China, it has misgivings about the direction of global politics under US unipolarity. Its political system is anathema to the West, and it jealously guards its sovereignty. In this context, we might expect the BRI to be a perfect stone with which to kill two birds: reduce US dominance in the region by supporting its enemy and secure China's energy supply and trade routes.

China made several announcements but many authors have found the promised $400 billion investment plan to be unrealistic (Garlick & Havlová 2021: 3). Not just that, China has actively (and successfully) courted Saudi Arabia, Iran's nemesis and increased imports of oil from the kingdom as it reduced its trade with Iran. As Garlick and Havlová continue, there can be only one answer to this puzzle: China is hedging its bets. Rather than challenge US military dominance, it is paying its dues and going to great lengths not to irritate the Americans over Iran. The BRI rhetoric may be going strong when it comes to Iran, but China is not putting its money where its mouth is. This explains why among all strands of the overland BRI, the Iran-bound belt is the least realized.

Elsewhere, in the Middle East, China has similarly avoided becoming entangled in the region's politics. Going against the conventional wisdom that would see an emerging superpower wanting to gain a foothold in the oil-rich and geostrategically important region, China has stayed clear of any military adventures and political interference. Although its involvement in economic development in the Middle East is growing and its dependence on oil is stronger than ever, China is comfortable with being a security free rider, benefiting from the military presence of the USA and, secondarily, Russia.

Chinese troops have stayed away from the Iraq wars, the operations against ISIS and the civil war in Syria and elsewhere. Its diplomatic effort in the Israeli–Palestinian conflict and the Syrian crisis are "feeble" at best (Evron 2019: 200). This approach has been described as attempting to maximize economic profits by being "everyone's friend" (*ibid.*) and for the time being has served China's energy security interests. Regarding the BRI, its expansion in the Middle East has been modest, given that it promotes connectivity in a region ridden by imperialism and conflict. However, this case also adds little evidence to support the idea that China is developing a military-security agenda as a component of the BRI.

If the BRI is a grand strategy to project China's military power across the wider Eurasian continent, it is not a particularly efficient one given its reliance on the autocratic regimes of Central Asia – not to mention it directly challenges Russia's appointed role as custodian of security in the region. Even though China offered security support during the Kazakhstan protests of January 2022, it was ultimately Russian "peacekeepers" that were dispatched under the Collective Security Treaty Organization's mandate. In Pakistan, the expansion of BRI-security is a costly affair relying on the cooperation of Pakistani security forces. The Libyan evacuation, as well as China's UN mission in South Sudan, elegantly foreshadowed the potential for entanglement that the BRI brings. China, whose insistence on non-interference in the sovereign affairs of other states is a mantra, is undoubtedly aware that projects in high-risk countries come with – high risk (Shen & Zhang 2018). But not every risk mitigation strategy may be compatible with China's foreign policy ideals and goals, nor is a one-size-fits-all strategy appropriate for the BRI's varied security landscape.

One last thing to consider is that regardless of whether China has the ambition to build a regional hegemonic order (and per Mearsheimer, use this as a foundation of global supremacy) or not, it faces a very different international environment to the 1940s and 1950s when the USA, the current hegemon, supplanted Britain as the world's dominant force. Historically minded international relations scholarship has put forward the "power transition theory" as one way to explain how a transition from one global hegemon to another takes place. Organski, who put forward the theory, outlines a string of hegemonic transitions following the line from Portugal to the Netherlands, Britain and finally the USA (Organski 1958). While the theory has been challenged on different grounds, one aspect remains relevant for our discussion: Organski notes that the *cost* of challenging a reigning hegemon has been increasing over time, making successful contestation extremely difficult. Indeed, the transition between Britain and the USA was almost consensual, considering Britain could hardly maintain its empire after two costly world wars and the end of colonialism.

China therefore faces an extremely tall order if its aim is to supplant the US hegemony. It is surrounded even in its region by powerful states such as Japan and India, an unpredictable Russia to its north and a string of US bases and allies surrounding its shores. The BRI does very little to change the balance of power in any of these. It defers to Russia in Central Asia, it aggravates the relationship with India over Pakistan and sets up a sort of competitive developmentalism with Japan in Southeast Asia and beyond. Its maritime component equally does not challenge US naval dominance, although it has the potential to significantly alter the balance of power in the Indian Ocean. Moreover, hegemons do not rule through military domination but rely on a network of mutually beneficial institutions that shape global relations in the hegemon's favour. As the section on norms demonstrates below, China still has a long way to go if it wants to supplant the US-centric liberal international order – although the Trump presidency has certainly made this objective less strenuous for China.

Lacking a hegemonic ambition or potential does not, however, mean that the BRI has no security aspect to it, quite the contrary. Increased economic and political ties between China and the world have already required China to drop several of its diplomatic norms: securing a permanent military base in Djibouti, organizing a military-led evacuation without a UN mandate, tackling the messy security picture in Pakistan all go against the non-interventionist maxims of Chinese foreign policy. It is therefore not inconceivable that, as the BRI progresses, more norms will be broken, loosened or redefined.

An area of interest in this regard is the emergence of Chinese private security companies (PSCs) in the global market of security services. The expansion of the BRI means growing security concerns around key projects and lines of connectivity, but its first decade has witnessed a rather shy growth of Chinese PSCs. Currently, there are around 20–40 Chinese security companies that operate abroad with approximately 3,000–4,000 personnel (Arduino 2018: 5; Markusen 2022: 3). Chinese law prohibits military contractors and places restrictions in the use of arms by PSCs. But their international presence has raised concerns over regulation and effective oversight that are similar to the notorious cases of Blackwater and the Wagner Group, US and Russian private military contractors, respectively, that became involved in massacres of civilians in the Middle East and Africa; and there are also fears surrounding the close relations between Chinese PSCs and PLA personnel, which may lead to the latter informally operating abroad (Peterson 2020). It remains to be seen whether the expanding economic interests of Chinese SOEs will drive overseas a new generation of PSCs that could resemble more military contractors such as Blackwater.

Lastly, as China becomes more active on the world stage, some of its existing relationships, which were founded on the promise of non-interference, may begin to strain, while others find new depth as concrete common goals are identified. China's relations with the developing world merit particular attention here. While it is unlikely China would be able to significantly alter the liberal world order, it may build a parallel set of international institutions in the parts of the world that have so far gained the least from the US-centric order. Such a coalition of the disgruntled could in turn begin to set the global agenda, as has already happened during climate change negotiations. Yet if the BRI is the main vehicle through which such a competitive world order could be realized, it will need more than just physical infrastructure and security aspects. It would need to be a foundation for a new normative order.

A NEW NORMATIVE ORDER?

The BRI has been interpreted as evidence that China is establishing a regional hegemony as the first step to its ascendancy in global power status. As already discussed, this argument is hard to sustain, given the absence of collective security arrangements in the region led by China, and that existing organizations (such as the SCO) create weak defence commitments. In addition, the PLA's provocative activities in the South China Sea are the product of ambition but also of weakness, as Chinese naval projection power capabilities remain limited beyond its periphery. Even if CCP leaders envisage regional hegemony, there is no clear path to achieving it. The US security commitments in East Asia (South Korea, Taiwan) have emerged stronger in the post-Trump era, Japan is a formidable and rearmed adversary, Association of Southeast Asian Nations (ASEAN) countries remain vigilant against Chinese military presence, while neither India nor Russia would tolerate the PRC's predominance in South and Central Asia, respectively. In this context, a radical reshuffling on the balance of power in China's periphery would possibly involve military confrontation, which remains a high-risk option for a regime that places its own survival above any other goal.

Any discussions on the nature and future of the BRI cannot escape this security context. However, scholars have identified yet another possible path for China to rise as a global power, through its norms and ideas about trade, diplomacy and cooperation in the economic field becoming dominant. The BRI's function in this regard is to increase China's gravitational power in the economic field, which will enhance its ability to remodel the normative context of global capitalism and international relations according to its own values and predispositions.

We can identify two broad traits in this argument. The first consists of cultural-civilizational explanations, which are popular in public discourse and rich in imagery but weak in empirical validation. According to these views, the Confucian tradition of the Sinocentric world has a direct impact on Chinese foreign policy-making that seeks to establish China as the normative centre of the world order. Imperial China had established a normative context for its relations with other states that was widely accepted in East Asia. At the heart of this context was the idea that the Chinese emperor was bestowed with the mandate to rule "all under heaven" (*tianxia*), which signified China's indisputable cultural superiority. This Sinocentric world order was institutionalized in the highly ritualistic tributary system that regulated trade and diplomacy with the Chinese empire, providing political benefits for the empire and substantial economic ones for the tributary states (Cohen 2001: 25). Nowadays, the argument goes, the traditional context takes a different form, but its core logic remains relatively unchanged:

> That element of Tianxia would in our time be represented by economic relations. Legally and politically, the states included in the Belt and Road would remain fully sovereign and independent. In practice, economic power would bind the system together and prevent it from falling apart. It is precisely in this informality that the initiative most obviously differs from the existing Western order which emphasizes legal and institutionalized procedures. The Belt and Road is

> not an entity with fixed rules; rather, it is deliberately intended
> to be informal, unstructured and opaque.
>
> (Maçães 2018: 35)

There is no doubt that referring to China's imperial past to describe its contemporary behaviour is a great storytelling technique. But the narrative is ahistorical and, as it fails to establish a causal explanation, ultimately resorts to stereotyping. China underwent a very difficult path of integration to the West-centric international system, during which nothing remained static. Ideas on civilizational superiority have become a part of nationalist self-imagination, the "national myth" serving the idea of the Chinese nation-state. Accordingly, China's understanding of international relations has long moved away from the tributary system, and its long pursuit of autonomy vis-à-vis imperialist, communist and capitalist overlords is well-entrenched in the normative context of an international community of sovereign nation-states. Nowadays, China's authoritarian government frequently refers to its imperial past and the Confucian tradition as a way to fill its ideological vacuum, legitimize its rule and advocate the "incompatibility" between western democracy and Chinese society.

But we should not take rhetoric at face value. After all, the futility of cultural-civilizational explanations of China's current foreign policy is made evident by the fact that the imperial tradition has been used by scholars to both prove China's hegemonic ambitions and diagnose its supposedly cultural aversion to pursuing hegemony (Yan 1995; Roy 1996). More than creating cultures of hegemony, what the BRI may be creating is a geopolitical culture that goes beyond elite understandings and begins to shape public conceptions through its spatial logic (Lin, Sidaway & Woon 2019: 510). In this reading, the BRI may not be a hegemonic project per se, but will nevertheless define the way in which Chinese actors think about the geopolitical space they inhabit. This thought-provoking rearticulation brings our attention back to how Chinese narratives of the BRI are not a neat given, but are rather an emergent phenomenon that we are observing in real time (*ibid.*), which is why our focus is driven by a grounded analysis of key projects and areas.

The second strand of arguments about China's normative challenge to the existing Asian and global orders concentrates on Beijing's ambition to leverage its economic power to create institutions that will render

China the norm-maker of international economic cooperation and diplomacy. As Hillman put it in his book on the BRI, Chinese economic actors here take on the role of the invaders:

> The BRI in its current form presents a different threat. The invaders are not massing at the EU's [European Union] borders with horses or tanks but strolling into European capitals with briefcases in hand. Yet China's influence, and its use of economic tools for political aims, has already caught the attention of European leaders. Even as they debate whether to become more like China in their responses, a consensus has emerged that China is not going to become more like the EU. (Hillman 2020: 97)

Rather than the outcome of an unspecified propensity harking back to its imperial past, this view understands the BRI as part of a broader grand strategy to "weave" neighbouring and faraway countries in a dense, Sinocentric network of "economic, political, cultural and security relations", that will allow China to emerge as a normative power, first regionally and then globally (Callahan 2016: 226–8). Multilateral forums and institutions led by China, such as the AIIB, function as the platform where participating states socialize with China's normative system, with the aim of adopting it as an alternative to the West-centred canon of global governance (*ibid.*: 237).

This is a compelling argument that draws our attention to the impact of the BRI outside the economic sphere. It also opens an alternative explanation of China's grand strategy, one that does not rely solely on military strength but gives emphasis to the effectiveness of its ideas about international cooperation, backed by dreams of no-strings-attached investment. The stated values of Chinese foreign policy and of the BRI – openness, inclusivity and emphasis on "win-win" cooperation – are translated into a model of policy coordination that respects sovereignty and places emphasis on infrastructural, financial and trade connectivity (Callahan 2016). This model is thought to be more appealing for developing nations than the conditionality-heavy international organizations that are often accused of exporting the western experience with development (Stone 2008; Kilby 2009; Stokke 2013).

Logical as this argument may sound, it does not capture the entire story. Taking the most important institutional offspring of China's global ambitions, the AIIB, as an example, we can see that global institutions created by China do not necessarily challenge the existing material or normative structure of international cooperation. The AIIB has been inclusive and accommodating of western countries, who have not only been encouraged to join but have been given leeway to influence its organizational design and operation (Knoerich & Urdinez 2019). The AIIB's experience so far is one of integration into the existing structure of global financial governance, not one of contestation. It is about increasing China's share of the multilateral financial pie, not serving everyone mooncakes instead. The AIIB has increased the number of projects that are co-funded with existing multilateral banks, where rules set by each of the banks need to be followed, creating not a lowest common denominator but rather a layering of lending practices. There is no doubt that China gains from the AIIB economically and, more importantly, increases its soft power and prestige as a rule-maker and contributor to global economic governance (Men 2018: 37–8), but this is very different from the narrative of China luring its neighbouring regions into accepting the normative hegemony of its distinct value system.

A second example is that of the 17+1 grouping. Eastern and central European countries were initially excited about the economic opportunities that China offered but, not even a decade in, a prevailing sense of disappointment has gripped the region, as lofty promises of investment turned out to be a mirage. As Turcsányi (2020) argues, Chinese promises found fertile ground after the post-2008 crisis, when Chinese investment was a welcome alternative to the perceived stinginess of the EU (deserved or not). The arrival of China was greeted in western Europe with suspicion and talk of Chinese "Trojan Horses" being created, an image that fit well into a larger narrative of China toppling the West from its hegemonic position. Here, we can identify an underlying (and possibly unintended) ahistorical determinism based on Mearsheimer's work on how superpowers rise, which follows the US experience of first hegemonizing its periphery and then projecting its force globally (2001).

But we would do well to remember the work of power transition theorists, who point out that the cost of successfully challenging a dominant power has risen considerably through modernity and that, in any case, a conflict is not unavoidable as long as the rising power is satisfied enough with the system it inhabits. While the BRI certainly complicates the balance of global power and influence, especially in the developing world, it is not clear whether it is the right vehicle to unseat the USA or supplant the liberal international order on which large parts of the BRI's building blocks rely.

NOT A GRAND STRATEGY?

The BRI is not a grand strategy aimed at securing China's hegemony. Any comparisons with the rise of the USA as a global power are more distorting than telling, while neither its security component nor its normative package constitute an aggressive defiance to the liberal international order. Economic interests create political ones, no doubt, but the alarmism often seen in public discourse reflects primarily the anxiety of some of China's competitors rather than the actual picture on the ground.

Yet the Initiative has given both domestic and global politics a focal point of discussion about a key topic – China's rise. As Xi Jinping ominously talked about "changes not seen in hundreds of years" (*bainian weiyouzhi dabianju* 百年未有之大变局, Xinhua: 2017) being afoot, the community of China watchers started to see in the BRI a long-awaited materialization of the CCP's hegemonic ambition. But as we have shown in this section, the BRI lacks the organizational, ideological and normative coherence to truly be the strategic masterpiece it is often claimed to be. Moreover, the ways in which the Initiative relates to China's security concerns further demonstrates that, for the CCP, domestic regime survival and economic development remain the key goals.

But this does not mean that the BRI and its predecessor policies and offshoots will not significantly alter the global balance of power or undermine certain tenets of the liberal international order. Being a strategy driven by China's state capitalist economy, the BRI thrives best in environments where Chinese SOEs feel at home. In this way the BRI has strengthened autocratic regime traits by pandering to strongmen from Malaysia to Montenegro who were keen to avoid transparency to suit their political goals. Moreover, the BRI itself is not even an accurate reflection of China's economy, because the BRI is almost entirely dominated by lumbering state enterprises. Unlike the Chinese economy, the input of private actors in the BRI is small, competition weak and funding sources readily available. To say the BRI spreads China's economic model is to misunderstand how China's economy has developed over the past decades. In some ways, the BRI combines the worst aspects of China's economy being exported outwards.

The BRI continues the CCP's long relationship with the state economy that dates back to the post-Maoist debates about how to reform the economy, a debate that gradualists won (Weber 2021). Far from being a totalitarian monolith, the successes of the CCP can be assigned largely to its capacity for gradual action that spreads blame, crowdsources ideas and responds to local conditions and demands. Yet throughout China's economic reform, questions remained over how to increase efficiency in the state sector, how to combine political control and economic autonomy. The BRI forms part of that mode of governance, addressing state sector weakness (overcapacity, low productivity, lack of internationalization) by harnessing state banks looking for healthy returns on investment.

But just as in China, the BRI will only find success where SOEs and host-state actors are allowed to experiment and find solutions that fit local contexts. This makes the BRI an unlikely candidate for a hegemonic strategy aimed at subjugating Asia (or even the world), because of the huge role SOEs have in shaping locally specific outcomes. This is precisely why, even though it is not a grand strategy, the BRI will have great repercussions for how China is bound to host states. Some of these bonds will be desired and beneficial to China, others unexpected and costly.

Whether intentional or not, the BRI has also struck a chord with developing states eager to move from vague and painstaking "capacity building" of western developmental lenders to the ribbon-cutting thrill of building big infrastructure. If the BRI is a danger to the international order, it is because China has successfully identified a global thirst for primary investment *without* normative undertones, particularly the reluctance to commit to principles of "lean, green and clean" infrastructure. In the following chapters, we leave behind the thrill of geopolitics and look at why the BRI has the potential for significant backsliding in the realms of environmental protection, transparency and social justice.

4

Is it green?

Xi Jinping often talks about the "green" BRI as a part of his vision for China's ecological civilization, which was outlined in the 2019 BRI Belt and Road Forum. In the words of the person tasked with instrumentalizing this vision, it establishes "a green consensus with BRI participating countries, strengthens cooperation on global biodiversity conservation, and moves together towards the 2050 vision of 'Living in Harmony with Nature' and pursues the goals of the UN's Agenda for Sustainable Development" (Xi 2019). Indeed, much of the discussion on "BRI 2.0" is centred around China's new commitments to sustainability (Ang 2019).

The BRI has so far created a small network of environmental initiatives: the BRI Green Development Coalition, the BRI Environmental Big Data Platform and the Green Silk Road Envoys Program that provides training for participating government officials. At the same time though, the BRI – a massive infrastructural initiative geared towards energy and transport sectors – is going to affect ecosystems from China to Chile. China's domestic environmental record is improving of late but only after decades of an outright war on nature in the pursuit of development (Watts 2010). This raises concerns about the capacity of various green "bolt-ons" to mitigate the sheer destructive power of rapid industrial development. The argument is convincing: if China failed to protect its own environment, why would Chinese companies be more environmentally minded elsewhere, especially in countries with weak regulatory systems (which abound on the Belt and Road)?

In some ways, this argument is unfair to China. Historically, economic development brought about environmental destruction, followed only later by the willingness and ability to repair some of the damage – a pattern known as the "environmental Kuznets curve" (named so after the more famous Kuznets curve correlating inequality and development). Following this line of reasoning, if the BRI brings about economic development in the "dirty" sectors of energy and transport, some environmental degradation is expected and would have happened anyway. We could also add that China's development was partly facilitated by the displacement of polluting industries from more developed economies, so it is not surprising that the West's dirty hand-me-downs are now being passed on to a new group of developers willing to trade the environment for industrial development.

Yet the BRI is unfolding under a different sky. With climate change and biodiversity loss at its worst, it may not be possible for future developers to follow the models of China, South Korea, Japan – or the West. China's role here is pivotal, yet unclear. Exactly how China's domestic "ecological civilization" will shape the environment of the Belt and Road is difficult to ascertain. As Tracy *et al.* put it, there is increasingly a schism between China's improving domestic environmental record and its questionable international one (Tracy *et al.* 2017).

How is China's economic and political engagement with the world going to affect the environment of the countries along the BRI? This chapter first analyzes why Belt and Road policies have *outcomes* that cause environmental degradation, for example through active displacement of polluting industries from China, or habitat loss caused by BRI projects. Second, it will look at the increase in *side effects* such as the spread of invasive species, carbon lock-in or increased emissions overall. Both outcomes and side-effects can be further elaborated into *material* and *normative* challenges to the environment. Material outcomes and side-effects change the environment itself, while the normative changes alter the way the environment is regulated and used.

Using these four parameters, we argue that the SOE-dominated nature of the BRI makes it more likely that the initiative will accelerate and amplify environmental destruction as well as a normative backsliding resulting in carbon lock-in and GDP-oriented growth strategies. Chinese SOEs have time and again proven to be untrustworthy custodians of the environment. Their quest for profit in mega-construction projects across the world is furthermore enabled by state-owned banks whose environmental policies are still in their infancy. While some of these

Table 4.1 How might the BRI cause environmental degradation?

	Outcomes	*Side-effects*
Material	➤ Pollution displacement	➤ Increased industrial emissions
	➤ Resource depletion	➤ Increased access to resources
	➤ Biodiversity loss	➤ Invasive species
Normative	➤ Insufficient EIA	➤ Carbon lock-in
	➤ "Campaign environmentalism"	➤ Ribbon-cutting fever
	➤ Weak rules on green audits of BRI finance	

risks are common to development, several among them were identified by a panel of interdisciplinary scientists as novel "frontier horizon
issues" that deserve particular attention due to their potential to grow
into huge problems down the line (Hughes *et al.* 2020). It is therefore
crucial to understand what, if any, institutional architecture exists to
mitigate some of the risks or neutralize some of the direct drivers of
environmental destruction, considering that existing transnational
environmental protection networks might not be able to cope with the
complexity, opacity and scale of the BRI.

MATERIAL OUTCOMES

The link between development and environmental destruction is not a
simple, lasting correlation. Although we have historically observed that
the destruction of nature follows economic development, industrialized
countries also have the capacity and political will to protect the environment and mitigate some of the losses accrued along the way. This is the
thinking behind the environmental Kuznets curve. Such a curve can be
observed in the industrialized countries of the West, yet the improvement of environmental conditions in the developed world came in the
wake of increasing pressure on resources and habitats globally.

This explains why many observers are worried that the BRI will displace pollution from China to less-developed countries. But that is not
all. China's record on upholding standards of environmental protection

is poor both at home and internationally. While western corporations might respond to pressure from public opinion, a free press and home regulators, it is unclear whether Chinese SOEs are subject to the same scrutiny, nor is it obvious who is tasked with punishing habitual violators overseas. Material outcomes of BRI policies must therefore be understood within the context of China's own record on environmental protection.

Rapid economic development in China has caused steep rises in its greenhouse gas emissions in the past decades, with per capita emissions quadrupling since 1990 (Ritchie & Roser 2020). China's environment, already under pressure from the Maoist model of economic development, came under a full-blown attack following economic reforms in 1978. The results were initially bleak: old forests logged into irreversible loss (Economy 2010: 64), Beijing's air pollution score literally breaking the scale in 2013 (Wong 2013) and around 80 per cent of underground water undrinkable by 2016 (Chen 2016). Yet in line with the expectations of the Kuznets curve, China has made big strides in reversing – or at least reducing – the rate of environmental destruction. Sticking to the three metrics of forest, air and water, only water pollution remains a severe problem, with reductions in industrial water pollution all but wiped out by increased agricultural wastewater (Ma *et al.* 2020). Once famous for its smog, Beijing has dropped out of the list of the world's 200 most polluted cities. Forest cover has also stabilized in recent years, mainly owing to a comprehensive ban on commercial logging in natural forests, introduced in April 2015.

But domestic victories now come with a global cost. The ban on commercial logging saw imports of timber immediately rise by 15 per cent (Zhang & Chen 2021) – and that is just the legally imported wood. Because China is one of the world's largest importers of illegal wood (Guan *et al.* 2020), the implications are clear: China's voracious appetite for resources, coupled with its efforts to combat environmental degradation domestically, are having significant knock-on effects around the world, especially in developing countries with weak regulatory systems. Illegal logging is one such unfortunate synergy, but the environmental outcomes of the BRI can be illustrated through three material drivers that bind China to its partners: *displacement* of pollution, *depletion* of resources and *destruction* of habitat and biodiversity.

Displacement of pollution

Displacement of polluting industries happens on the BRI in two ways: either through a direct relocation of Chinese industries to countries on the Belt and Road (analyzed here through the cement industry in Central Asia), or through increased lending and investment into the industrial sectors of host countries (illustrated by the example of coal power plants in Pakistan, Vietnam and the Balkans). Both ways are direct outcomes of domestic policy shifts, as well as the BRI's overarching emphasis on large infrastructure. Pollution displacement within the BRI is somewhat different to the displacement of polluting industries from western economies from the 1980s onwards. While the latter was driven by the globalization of production driven by market impulses, de-unionization, and trade liberalization, "China's globalization" has always had a strong state-led component, as we have explained in the previous chapters of this book. This does not mean the activities of Chinese enterprises internationally are all centrally planned but, rather, that many state actors pitch in towards centrally set goals and aims, while trying to avoid any political red lines and maximize their own bottom line.

This poses an interesting question for the "pollution haven hypothesis" that claims companies are attracted to locations with lax environmental rules in pursuit of profits. The hypothesis remains controversial, with plenty of evidence in support and against the notion. The hypothesis must be adjusted in China's case, however, because SOEs are not responding only to market signals but are also trying to catch the wind of state policies in their sails. In China's case, the state *is* the ultimate "market signal" for industry. Whether or not Chinese heavy industry is attracted to countries with lax environmental regulation is therefore a moot point – they are encouraged to go there anyway as part of the BRI. The cement industry is an explicit case of a state-sponsored displacement of polluting industries, revealing the acute environmental challenges stemming from the relocation of China's dirty industry over its borders, using the BRI as a conduit for investment and a convenient political cover.

Cement, a mixture of inorganic binders such as lime or calcium silicate, is a key ingredient of concrete and a companion of infrastructural development, so it is no wonder China produces more cement than any other country – by an enormous margin. An oft-quoted statistic by Vaclav Smil says China produced more cement in the three years from 2008 to 2010 than the USA used in the entire twentieth century (Smil 2013: 91). Amazingly, this statement appears to be correct. Even accounting for changes in construction techniques (less steel, more concrete) and preferred housing materials (wood and brick in the USA, concrete in China), this factoid vividly illustrates the size of China's cement industry. Even a relatively small shift of Chinese cement production overseas could double or triple cement output in certain BRI countries, bringing with it sharp increases in the usage of water, sand and electricity, as well as a rise in emissions and particulates. Cement alone contributes an astounding 7 per cent of global anthropogenic emissions of CO_2 (Liu, Zhang & Wagner 2018: 275), making it one of the key sources of greenhouse gas emissions. The production of cement is furthermore highly polluting in immediate surroundings, kicking up large amounts of fine dust. In China, for example, cement production accounts for 26.2 per cent of all particulates and 14.8 per cent of the total national CO_2 production (Chen, Hong & Xu 2015: 67).

Not only is China the biggest producer of cement in human history, it has recently become a large source of investment for cement production in its immediate neighbourhood. Vietnam is already the world's top exporter of cement, with China buying half of its annual exports (Global Cement 2021). Chinese researchers have identified a further 18 countries along the BRI as having significant potential for increased "cooperation" in cement production, forecast to triple from just under 20 million tons yearly in 2019 to over 60 million tons in 2023 (Sun & Chen 2019). In this context, the term "cooperation" denotes Chinese outward FDI, particularly by state-owned enterprises.

However, 60 million tons pales in comparison with China's installed production capacity of around 1.4 billion tons per year, but the trend is clear. Megaprojects such as the Rogun Dam in Tajikistan are behind rapid increases in Chinese-backed cement factories in the country, where production has increased five-fold since 2010 (Tracy *et al.* 2017: 77). As China scales back its cement production, especially in places with air pollution problems such as the northeast, so it becomes an importer of cement from the region and an exporter of capital for new production facilities (Global Cement 2022). Shangfeng, a cement producer from Hangzhou, for example, received a $68 million loan from the China Exim bank to increase production in Kyrgyzstan and Uzbekistan, while Chinese cement giants such as Gezhouba are also building plants for western cement multinationals such as LafargeHolcim (Gordeyeva & Goh 2019).

The cement industry is a harbinger of the potential for outsourcing polluting industries from China, facilitated by improved infrastructure in BRI countries. This dislocation is not only an environmental problem but also a political one. The Russian far east has already seen local population angered by Chinese government proposals to relocate metallurgical, cement and chemical plants from China's northeast. Russia's Ministry of the Development of the Far East replied that the concerns over this are unwarranted, as any projects would have to abide by Russia's own "stringent" regulations, but many environmentalists in the region are unconvinced by Moscow's assurances and point out that special development regions are already exempt from many strict rules (Shvarts & Fedichkina 2016). We return to the issue of host-state environmental regulation in the section on direct normative impacts and will instead continue here with the problem of natural resource depletion caused by the development of infrastructure.

Depletion of resources

Depletion of resources is an outcome affecting the environment all along the BRI. The example of cement and concrete production is once again a good case through which to explain the environmental impact of the BRI because both processes are very resource- and energy-intensive. To make cement and concrete, you need water and extract sand and gravel in large quantities. Being cheap but heavy, they are impractical to transport, so it is normally best to source them near construction sites. This is worrying because many BRI projects cluster in areas that are arid (such as Central Asia), have ecologically rich limestone karst regions (such as Southeast Asia) or are biodiversity hotspots (Southeast Asia,

East Africa, the Amazon, Ecuador). These fragile but globally significant ecosystems have become a tempting source of raw material for nearby construction sites.

Water-stress levels in Central Asia are already very high. The Soviet agricultural legacy lives on through inefficient irrigation and over-use of resources that has so far caused the dramatic disappearance of the Aral Sea, cross-border water conflicts, the drying out of Amu Darya and widespread soil salinification (Li *et al.* 2020: 2). The crisis has been compounded by above-average warming in the mountains of Tianshan that feed much of the region's water supply, causing the melting of glaciers and loss of sustainable glacial water resources (Chen *et al.* 2018). Projected population growth and temperature rises will exacerbate the already dire situation, so it is crucial that the region embarks on mitigation strategies now, to prevent disaster in the future.

Sadly, the "concrete and steel" character of the BRI is not a likely vehicle for such a transformation. Water management, while improving of late, is still an issue even in China proper, especially in regard to hydroelectric dams and agricultural water pollution. Moreover, China's actions in the wider Mekong River basin do not inspire confidence when it comes to sustainability and engagement with grassroots or international organizations. There, China's massive dams have caused environmental damage and economic suffering downstream, holding and redirecting water for China's own use under a shroud of secrecy; China's water usage data is considered a state secret (Eyler 2020). Now, countries downstream are rushing to build their own dams to regain some control over the flow of the river – dams that are, ironically, built by Chinese SOEs, using loans from Chinese banks.

The attention given to monumental dams and a tendency towards elite-level planning with little regard to complex interdependencies and trade-offs (Matthews & Motta 2015) certainly does not bode well. The BRI, by providing a domestic incentive for SOEs to go and seek work abroad, will only increase pressure on water resources, potentially replicating the problems China has at home. A review of water-related risks in Central Asia emphasizes four areas of concern: infrastructural development negatively affecting soil and water systems, industrial development causing water contamination and resource depletion, hydropower development to support infrastructure and industry, and agricultural use of water as part of China's agricultural engagement abroad (Davies & Matthews 2021: 6–11).

The intersections between China's voracious appetite for the world's resources and large infrastructure projects are not limited to its immediate region. The now cancelled string of mega-dams in Brazil, known as the São Luiz do Tapajós project, would have supplied electricity and reduced production costs for Brazilian soy exports to China by linking the remote farms of the Mato Grosso region with the seaport of Belem (Amazon Watch 2016). The Chinese SOE that would have built the dams, China Three Gorges Corporation, is Brazil's sixth-largest power operator since its acquisition of a stake in Portugal's EDP, while a different Chinese power company, State Grid, has won the contract to build a 2,100km-long power line to connect another environmentally problematic dam, Belo Monte, to Brazil's electric grid (Dialogo Chino 2016).

Many construction companies, Chinese or not, have been involved in scandals involving environmental and labour issues in Brazil, as well as the thorny issue of projects infringing of indigenous land. Yet what sets Chinese companies apart is the relatively hands-off approach of their main financier, China Export-Import Bank. Although Chinese financial groups have issued sector-wide guidance in coordination with the then Ministry of Environmental Protection (Foreign Economic Cooperation Office, Ministry of Environmental Protection 2017), these rules are not always applied on the ground, according to regional environmentalists (Amazon Watch 2016). This means Chinese SOEs are under less pressure from their financial backers to comply with either domestic, international or host-state norms on managing natural resources.

In a similar vein, the Coca Codo Sinclair hydroelectric dam in Ecuador displays a concerning number of direct effects on the surrounding environment, many of which could have been prevented with better resource management. The list of issues includes deforestation, improper waste removal impacting domestic water supplies, changes in subterranean run-off, fluctuations in water flows, sediment levels and flood patterns, as well as threats to flora and fauna in the surrounding Cayambe-Coca National Park and Sumaco Natural Reserve (Casey & Krauss 2018). That the dam is also a subject of a corruption scandal, explored in the next chapter, does not help with the perception that Chinese-funded megaprojects generate.

Lastly, the construction of massive infrastructures also exerts pressure on other local resources. While steel components are often made far away from their point of use, concrete by its nature tends to be sourced from relatively mundane materials in the vicinity of construction: water, sand, gravel. In Southeast Asia in particular, sand and gravel necessary for construction are taken from limestone-based karst areas. These ecological hotspots are already under pressure, annually shrinking by about 6 per cent in Southeast Asia – mainly due to extraction for concrete production (Hughes *et al.* 2020: 585). If we extrapolate future cement and concrete production from estimates about BRI-related production increases, the rate of loss could accelerate significantly.

Destruction of biodiversity

Destruction of biodiversity is another direct, material outcome of the BRI's specific trinity of transportation networks, energy infrastructure and industrial development. China's global presence could have taken form in many different ways but the emphasis on infrastructural connectivity was a choice that is intrinsically linked to the BRI. Among some of the global biodiversity hotspots affected by the BRI are Southeast Asia, the mountains of Central Asia, the coastal forests of East Africa, the Caucasus, the wider Mediterranean basin, the Amazon and the Himalayas (Lechner, Chan & Campos-Arceiz 2018).

What is worse, many of the areas that represent maximum diversity and house many of the region's endangered and threatened species are near proposed routes for infrastructural development (Hughes 2019: 888). Loss of habitat and the degradation of forests are just the first in a series of interrelated risks that include aspects of increased extraction and access (mining, logging, hunting, poaching), roadkill and fragmentation of habitats into ever smaller patches. With as many as 60 per cent of key biodiversity areas and nearly 7 per cent of protected areas within 50km of rail development (*ibid.*: 887), the direct impact on biodiversity could be severe without well-planned mitigation strategies, which are not yet part of the BRI ethos. And even if they were, the complex picture on the ground resists the systemic, top-down environmentalism of the CCP kind. Solutions that worked in China may not work in Ecuador or Ethiopia. As Hughes found, different routes pose different types of risks to different types of flora and fauna, and levels of protection vary from state to state. Moreover, as we show in the following section, environmental impact assessments (EIAs) – of which there are very few! – should consider not just the most direct consequences of infrastructural development but ought to encompass the many correlated side-effects stemming from increased access to previously isolated areas.

MATERIAL SIDE-EFFECTS

Not all the BRI's material effects can be traced directly to its projects, nor are they strictly limited to areas immediately adjacent to them. More than individual projects themselves, the BRI as a whole will facilitate new modes of development that will have long-lasting effects on the economies and ecologies along its route. As such, we can expect certain unforeseen side-effects emerging, especially those stemming from the BRI's focus on creating new transnational linkages, such as increased economic activity and access to previously remote locations. Moreover, what differentiates side-effects from direct outcomes is that many of the former are unexpected knock-on effects of China's domestic policies unrelated to the BRI, but which nonetheless reverberate down the newly created links between China and the world, where the BRI acts as a conduit. None of the side-effects ever figure in the glossy maps showcasing big infrastructural projects, yet all the examples listed below contribute to a drastic material change in the environmental conditions of BRI states. Starting with the unexpected effects of a domestic crackdown on cryptocurrency, we examine how the opening up of previously untouched swathes of Eurasia has already led to increased logging and sand harvesting of both legal and illegal types.

A recent move of energy-hungry cryptocurrency mining operations from China to Central Asia encapsulates how China's domestic politics affect the world and can cause an *increase in emissions* beyond the narrow confines of the BRI. The "mining" of cryptocurrencies such as bitcoin is a computationally demanding activity that requires specialized computers to work 24/7, consuming huge amounts of electricity. Bitcoin mining consists of solving complex mathematical puzzles in order to verify transactions, but also rewards miners with a chunk of newly created coin, making it a lucrative activity where China was a long-time world leader. In 2019, as much as 75 per cent of the global bitcoin mining energy consumption took place in China (CCAF n.d.), while the total world emissions from bitcoin mining equalled those of the Czech Republic (Jiang *et al.* 2021). Considering the high demand for electrical power, digital mining operations in China would often be set up next to hydropower dams or coal power plants, taking advantage of off-peak electricity at cut-rate prices and even migrating seasonally across China's provinces in search of cheap power.

But cryptocurrency, with its decentralized structure that governments cannot easily control, is unsurprisingly not popular with the CCP, which moved to ban first trading and, subsequently, the mining of cryptocurrencies such as bitcoin on Chinese soil. From comprising the aforementioned 75 per cent of global energy consumption, China's mining operations had all but ceased long before the 2022 cryptocurrency crash. Where did the mining operations go? Just as Chinese mining started dying down from January 2021, the Cambridge Bitcoin Electricity Consumption Index detected a quadrupling of mining-related consumption of power in Kazakhstan, the USA and Canada.

While some of the operations in the USA do take advantage of cheap renewable power, many Chinese bitcoin mining operators moved to Kazakhstan. Two major operators, for example, moved to a specially built location in Ekibastuz, near the Kazakh–Russian border, that is powered by a nearby coal power plant. With only 1 per cent of Kazakhstan's energy mix coming from renewables, any significant migration of economic activity such as cryptocurrency mining will also increase its carbon emissions. The rapid increase in power consumption has led the Kazakh government to step in with hastily drafted limits to the activities of these digital miners (Bloomberg 2021). It is not clear where the displaced bitcoin mining industry will ultimately settle, but increases were detected not only in Kazakhstan but other BRI countries as well, showing how the fate of their energy security has become bound to China's in ways that follow increased connectivity due to the BRI.

The same increase in connectivity also impacts *access to natural resources* along the BRI routes. Several of the land-based "belts" cut through old-growth forests, most notably in Southeast Asia and on the

Sino-Russian border. Forests and other complex ecosystems are known to be affected by infrastructural development through a process of "fragmentation". As old forests get cut up into smaller patches by an evolving transportation network, each small piece is now a much less resilient ecosystem. A seminal study spanning over three decades looked at the impact of fragmentation in the Amazonian Forest and confirmed that such fragments are more susceptible to external shocks (Laurance *et al.* 2011). In the case of the Russian far east, oil and gas pipelines contribute to this fragmentation, adding to the mix their own risks such as oil spills, which, although rare, have a high impact when they do occur (Teo *et al.* 2019: 10).

The economic development and transportation networks that will result from the BRI will open old-growth forests to rapid increases in exploitation. Here too the link with Chinese domestic policy stands out: when China moved to ban logging and exploitation of old-growth forests, illegal logging increased in the Russian far east in the 2000s. Chinese nationals engaged in illegal logging in Russia with at least some complicity of local authorities, using fake or inappropriate licences, falsifying export quantities or logging in protected areas and felling protected trees (Ryzhova & Ioffe 2009: 358). At one point, many of the wooden products sold in Walmart stores in the USA, such as toilet seats or cribs, were made of wood illegally logged in Russia by Chinese firms (Khatchadourian 2008).

Increased construction rates and easier access in BRI areas have furthermore been linked to pressure on "common-pool" resources such as sand. Sand, often overlooked but always essential, is considered a common-pool resource because controlling access to it would be more costly than the resource itself. But although we think sand may be plentiful worldwide (statistics are almost non-existent), it can become depleted locally as extraction rates exceed those of natural replenishment through river flow. In Southeast Asia, the side-effect of China's economic development is twofold: dams reduced the flow of new sedimentary material from upstream, while BRI-related economic activity increased consumption of sand downstream. Unlike forests or water use, little reliable data exists about sand usage in Southeast Asia, but we know increasing pressures on this once abundant material in the region are linked with spikes in demand from China and Singapore (Torres *et al.* 2017). The resulting depletion of sand locally (often as a consequence of illegal dredging done under the cover of night) has led to the erosion of river banks, increased flood risks, habitat loss and increased risks of malaria outbreaks (Torres *et al.* 2017).

It is not only humans and their goods that use new transport networks though. *Invasive species* have long been associated with the transnational movement of people and goods. The risk posed by invasive species that might hitch a ride to a new ecosystem is a major cause of the loss of biodiversity. The way in which biodiversity loss through invasive species occurs is largely dependent on the invaders' suitability to the new habitats, but also on the introduction risks and the fragility of the "target" ecosystem itself. Using these metrics, several surveys point out that the BRI has an exceptionally high risk of introducing invasive species into fragile biodiversity hotspots that are a good match for the invasive species. A study by Liu *et al.* (2019: 500–502) identified 14 areas susceptible to the spread of non-native terrestrial vertebrate species across the world, including swathes of Chile, much of eastern and southern Europe, the Maghreb, parts of South and Southeast Asia and the Pacific and New Zealand.

Nor are the dangers of invasive species limited to the critters that we can see: in the landmark "Horizon Scan" of BRI risks, the spread of "invisible" invasive species (fungi, bacteria, viruses) was identified as a key risk to human health and, more plausibly, food security. While not many microbial organisms can harm humans directly, quite a few have the potential to severely impact our diets and reliance on organic resources (Hughes *et al.* 2020). While we reflect on the impact of the Covid-19 pandemic in the conclusion of the book, it would be remiss not to point out the potential for pathogens to travel and also that the spread of disease along the BRI has direct repercussions for the feasibility of many of the BRI's projects.

From sand and timber to intangible digital currencies and invasive species big or small, the BRI is a network that binds the world's fate to China's domestic policies, establishing trade and production networks that are not always beyond reproach. This is a consequence of regulatory weaknesses in China, the host BRI states, as well as end markets such as the USA or Europe. This link is particularly worrisome in areas that are already experiencing increased environmental pressures, such as Southeast and Central Asia. To ensure the BRI does not only export damaging industries and deplete resources, a stronger normative framework around the role of environment protection within BRI countries is necessary, yet Chinese actors have in many ways fallen short of their own goals, contributing instead to several instances of normative backsliding across the BRI.

NORMATIVE OUTCOMES

After years of rapid industrial development, China ended up in an environmental morass where, as Elizabeth Economy's eponymous book said, "the river ran black". Already subjected to the stresses of Maoist developmental logic, the environment in China did not figure very high on the agenda of the CCP. Until the damage started to undermine its legitimacy and appearance of competence, that is. As environmental protests spread and mobilized the now affluent middle classes, the party decided it was time to clean up its act. The Chinese authorities have since made great strides in improving the level of environmental protection domestically, relying on the tried and tested mixture of administrative decrees, campaigns and party discipline that now make up its environmental policy toolbox. Yet what remains sorely lacking are truly independent means of verifying compliance and punishing infractions, which are simply not suited to the political landscape of a one-party authoritarian state. If an independent agency or a free press existed to scrutinize environmental performance, the logic goes, it would not take long before they started asking questions about other politically sensitive issues.

Why are environmental norms in China relevant to the activities of Chinese actors internationally? If China's domestic push to protect nature relies on *campaign environmentalism*, we need to understand whether the impact of such campaigns reaches beyond Chinese borders at all. Campaigns are a trusty policy tool in the arsenal of the CCP, having been used to great effect (and great tragedy) since the beginnings of the PRC. Best described as a flurry of bureaucratic activity, campaigns can achieve set targets in surprising time and are a testament to the power of the Chinese state and party. Yet campaigns also suspend daily norms, replacing the less exciting work of monitoring compliance with eye-catching targets for the planting of trees, reduction of smog or the greening of vehicles across China's cities.

Most importantly in our case, however, campaigns rely heavily on the presence of the party in all walks of social and political life: a presence that can direct, incentivize and verify whether bureaucratic and company activity is contributing to the goals of a campaign. When SOEs are conducting their business in other countries, though, the pressures exerted by the CCP are not always felt as acutely. They must also learn to deal with local stakeholders who do not answer to the call of the party's historic mission but are instead motivated by the immediate material gains on offer. The fundamental difference is that Chinese actors and their local hosts do not always share normative viewpoints, nor are they bound by the same rules and practices. Thus, environmentalism with Chinese characteristics is not suited to the international nature of the BRI, resulting in less than ideal normative outcomes; to name but two: inadequate EIAs in the pre-construction stage, and insufficient environmental audits of financing for BRI projects by state-owned banks.

EIAs have been advancing in scope and use in China since the very first one was conducted in 1979. While the process is still flawed (Wang, Morgan & Cashmore 2003; Zhang 2016), the consolidation of domestic standards is a priority issue for Xi Jinping's political goal of "blue sky, green mountains and clear rivers". Despite domestic achievements, many BRI projects have EIAs that are non-existent or flawed. References to EIAs or other environmental reviews are only rarely featured in BRI policy (Tracy *et al.* 2017) and the effectiveness of EIAs on the ground varies greatly.

Since it is impractical to evaluate every single BRI project, a study by Aung, Fischer and Shengji (2020) instead chose to evaluate environmental standards and practices across 49 countries participating in the BRI. The results suggest that much of the BRI funding flows to countries with low scores; that is, destinations with weak or wholly inappropriate environmental protection norms, among which we find some BRI stalwarts such as Kyrgyzstan, Kazakhstan, Laos, Mongolia, Montenegro, Serbia and Turkmenistan. On the other hand, among BRI destinations with the highest EIA scores, some, such as Slovenia or Poland, host very little BRI investment, while others such as Vietnam or Malaysia are zones of major BRI activity.

The study therefore does not support the so-called "pollution haven" hypothesis, since investment into jurisdictions with stringent rules does happen on a large scale as well. On the other hand though, the results tell us that, given China's own vague and non-binding rules, the level of regulatory control over the environmental impact of BRI projects is largely dependent on the *host* countries' capacity and political will. Quite often Chinese loans are the only available financing option for politically important projects in states with no access to capital markets (Shen & Zhang 2018). In such cases, host states are naturally disincentivized from making life hard for their Chinese partners, preferring instead to open doors for them and smooth out any "bureaucratic" obstacles such as EIAs (Tsimonis *et al.* 2019; Rogelja 2020).

The onus is thus on the Chinese authorities to incentivize SOEs and lenders to generate positive normative outcomes that will build up local capacity rather than take advantage of flexible regimes. A key node where this might be achieved is in strengthening *weak regulation on green finance.* Indeed, reputational risks to the BRI have spurred the Chinese government to react by issuing new environmental guidelines to Chinese entities overseas. Some measures to ensure compliance and reporting by Chinese companies working abroad pre-date the BRI but, since 2012, we have seen a focus on the environmental performance of companies working in BRI countries, suggesting that the greening of the BRI is definitely on the government's agenda.

Starting with banks that finance BRI projects, the China Banking and Insurance Regulatory and Commission issued in 2012 its first "Green Credit Guidelines", which remain, with updates, the most important piece of regulation sustaining green lending (Coenen *et al.* 2021). The guidelines were meant to nudge banks towards greener lending practices by encouraging them to develop environmental risk assessment capacities, strengthen due diligence and compliance monitoring, as well as invest into green banking policies and managerial reviews (China Banking and Insurance Regulatory Commission 2012). The regulation could be deemed a success because it stimulated the creation of environmental policies in all the major policy banks that sustain Chinese overseas lending. Yet, simultaneously, we know that banks such as China Exim continue to finance environmentally damaging projects with inadequate EIAs and shaky financial prospects. Chinese banks may have produced a wealth of policies, guidelines and managerial capacities but they still lack the resolve to enforce rules, monitor compliance and punish infractions (Losos *et al.* 2019).

Much of the confusion about China's norms for green financing stems from the misunderstanding of what mandatory or voluntary disclosure rules mean for Chinese firms. Despite the proliferation of legislation, in practice there are no mandatory rules for public disclosure of environmental information to the public, and only the party-state has the influence and power to force compliance when it wants to (Hui & Tilt 2018).

As long as the state refuses to meaningfully punish environmentally reckless SOEs, we are back to square one: relying on a watchful international public and free press to identify and pressure companies with poor environmental records to improve their practices. This can take place by pressuring local supporters, as was the case in several successful campaigns such as the one against the Lamu coal power plant in Kenya (Dahir 2019). Alternatively, direct action can be targeted at Chinese companies in the hope of raising reputational costs and perhaps even stirring the Chinese state into action.

A recent case that supports this view is the Batang Toru hydropower dam project on the island of Sumatra in Indonesia. Environmentalists vehemently opposed the project because it would endanger the habitat of the Tapanuli orangutan, the world's rarest great ape. Indonesian environmental group WALHI then sent an open letter to the Bank of China, which was expected to finance the project (WALHI 2019). Months later, it received a terse reply saying the bank will "evaluate the project". Although the Bank of China has reportedly withdrawn from financing the dam, construction continues on site (Simangunsong 2021).

The opaque way in which many of the BRI projects are financed make it difficult for small environmental groups to even know who to target, let alone bring to a grinding halt the vast machinery of concessionary loans, political interests and tempting kickbacks. Without an earnest commitment by China, some projects may be stopped but many others will be built regardless of the cost to the environment, underscoring the importance of strong normative standards in China proper.

NORMATIVE SIDE-EFFECTS

China is the world's biggest investor in renewable energy. Even if we discount hydropower, which can be highly destructive to river ecosystems, China's commitment to solar and wind power industries has brought about economies of scale and a reduction in the price of renewables, while the push to electrify transport has resulted in such memorable inventions as the e-sanlunche and other inexpensive vehicles ideal for developing country conditions. It is entirely feasible that more of such clean technology will travel down the BRI – it already has in some cases.

Improvements and upgrades to existing coal power plants have taken place in Central Asia (Teo *et al.* 2019), in the Balkans (Rogelja 2020) as well as Latin America and Southeast Asia (Li, Gallagher & Mauzerall 2020). While Chinese capital does finance (by a slim majority) newer supercritical coal power plants rather than subcritical ones, even newer coal plants are a significant source of greenhouse gases despite their more efficient running and lower emissions of SO_2 and NO_2 in particular. Moreover, the BRI in particular seems to attract less renewables investment from China than non-BRI countries (*ibid.*). This could be because BRI countries on the whole are developing countries, while Chinese investments into more expensive renewables tend to happen in the developed world. If we add the amount of export credits and other loans that are not direct investments, the predominance of coal in the BRI grows even larger, suggesting that the BRI might be contributing to a carbon lock-in for many of the countries relying on Chinese loans and SOEs to expand their power production.

Carbon lock-in will delay any decarbonization efforts through a combination of sunk investment into fossil fuels and the resulting empowerment of political actors dependent on a carbon-intensive economy at the expense of renewables. A carbon lock-in is a particularly stubborn form of path dependency because of the large capital costs and long lives of infrastructure (Seto *et al.* 2016). We illustrate how this normative side-effect works in the case of southeast Europe. Situated on the doorstep of the EU, which exerts a substantial normative influence on Balkan countries, this region is a convenient test site to evaluate the repercussions of BRI financing for fossil fuel energy. Unlike many Global South countries, Balkan states on the whole have the financial, technical and political capacities for a shift towards sustainable energy generation, yet have repeatedly failed to make significant efforts to wean themselves off coal power in particular.

Southeast Europe is blessed (or cursed) with some of the largest reserves of lignite coal in Europe. Lignite is a heavy fuel with low energy density and is, moreover, prone to spontaneous combustion when piled up. It is in many regards almost the opposite of oil – its use is predominately limited to geographically proximate electricity and heat production. Being found at shallow depths, it is also a cheap and plentiful fuel, creating a tempting combination of incentives despite its negative effect on the environment – both during excavation and combustion. This context is important in structuring the nature of China's coal financing in the region. Significant lignite mines and associated power plants were already present in the region, so China is not changing the energy mix on which southeast European countries rely; rather, it is helping to perpetuate it by changing the political calculus necessary for a transition to cleaner fuel. With most of the Chinese-built plants scheduled to operate for the next three decades, this building spree will lock countries such as Bosnia-Herzegovina and Serbia into a high-emissions future. This is particularly concerning since both already rely very heavily on coal-powered electricity generation (Bosnia 68 per cent and Serbia 69 per cent – IEA Electricity Information 2018).

Chinese banks and contractors are currently involved in the installation, planning or pre-planning of a total of 2,180MW of generating power worth over €3 billion across the two countries – all of which is from lignite-based thermoelectric plants. Some 650MW of coal-powered plants are already operational or under construction, a further 450MW in advanced planning and permission stage, while the remaining 1,080MW are in early stages of development (Rogelja 2020). These numbers represent only a fraction of China's global coal financing, estimated at around €44 billion by Global Energy Monitor (2022), and it is unclear whether Xi's pledge to stop global coal financing will cripple any projects already in development, or how far back the pipeline this pledge will reach. Rather, the point is that even in the vicinity of a legislative and normative behemoth such as the EU, the allure of new coal power plants bankrolled by China proved too tempting to refuse.

Western Balkan states are "milking" their coal power plants as long as possible (Simon 2021), and it is Chinese financing via the BRI that is extending the realms of what is politically and economically possible when it comes to coal in Europe. The dividing line between EU members and non-EU countries in the Balkans is stark. While union members Croatia and Greece committed to kicking their coal habits, non-members such as Bosnia found themselves in a position to sell their excess power to the same EU member states, as is already the case with one Chinese-built facility in the country. The gamble that western Balkans states are taking is as follows: build coal power plants now, sell dirty power to the EU and then hope exceptions and mitigation plans will be made for their decommissioning in the future.

The BRI's role in this is to not only delay decarbonization but to shift the incentive structure of the host countries' domestic political calculus towards a *ribbon-cutting fever*, where the competence of government is increasingly measured in the kilowatts of power generation, miles of railroad and number of twenty-foot equivalent units (TEUs) carried over in ports. Here it is particularly important to underline the role of geostrategic considerations by the USA, Japan and the EU as the main sources of competitive credit and expertise for large infrastructural projects in the developing world. All three have of late become involved in a global competition with China, vying for limited public funds in the Global South with ever-new initiatives and incentives.

Japan's high-speed rail industry has, for example, engaged in open competition with that of China; both countries consider high-speed rail a flagship export technology, with Southeast Asia presenting an especially interesting target market (Pavlićević & Kratz 2017). During the course of their rail rivalry, both countries aggressively supported their bids by loosening financial feasibility calculations, thus increasing the chance of unnecessary and potentially environmentally unsound megaprojects being built on the back of this competition.

The EU's "Global Gateway" initiative, which aims to mobilize €300 million in investments between 2021 and 2027, will equally have to contend with the dangers of building large infrastructures just to prove a geopolitical point, regardless of the impact on the environment. Competition between global giants may be beneficial to developmental elites from Serbia to Sri Lanka, but such a fevered atmosphere might not consider the interests of sustainable development and environmental protection.

A GREEN FUTURE FOR THE BRI?

The BRI has huge potential to change the lives of millions living along its vaguely defined routes but it is likely to do so alongside huge and irreversible environmental destruction. The present chapter has surveyed scientific literature, which, although retaining some measured optimism, by and large agrees on the severity of risks posed by rapid industrial development of the Chinese model.

The BRI's bias towards big infrastructural projects built by SOEs means the Initiative as a whole is likely to produce both material and normative shifts in how the environment of BRI countries is exploited, affected and regulated. First, there are the almost unavoidable costs to the environment stemming from increased industrial development. Balancing sustainability with development is difficult and we can hardly begrudge the desire for economic development that is a goal for many developmental regimes along the BRI. But as we have shown, China's role here is not only to facilitate development but to facilitate development of a certain kind. The norms that travel overseas with Chinese contractors do not inspire confidence. Faulty EIAs, banks that turn a blind eye, corrupt regimes that care more for the bottom line than biodiversity or clean air.

To improve on its environmental record so far, China will have to first strengthen the normative provisions for its overseas activities. The signals from the top are somewhat encouraging. Xi used his UN address in September 2021 to pledge a stop to coal financing abroad. The details of the pledge are not clear yet, but the direction of travel has been set. While China's commitments on coal internationally are not formally part of its nationally determined contributions under the Paris Agreement, a similar "ratcheting up" of targets could happen in the BRI as well, as each pledge brings with it higher reputational costs if promises are broken. But the BRI, unlike China's domestic pledges, is a complex playing field with many different actors. While the BRI is furthering physical connectivity, it is doing less well in terms of environmental regulation, which remains fragmented.

An integrated environmental management strategy that includes transnational stakeholders would be a solution to the coordination and regulatory alignment issues that plague the BRI, but such an arrangement is unpalatable to a regime that is obsessive about protecting its sovereignty. China's actions in the Mekong River basin suggest it is open to multilateral reciprocity – but on its own terms. China has shunned the Mekong River Commission because it sees it as too affected by outside – western and non-governmental organization (NGO) – influence and has put forward its own multilateral initiative, the Lancang–Mekong Cooperation. China's preference for state-level multilateralism thus precludes meaningful engagement by non-state bodies, leaving it and the various host states as the only stakeholders – a coalition that has so far delivered a lot of coal power plants, bridges to nowhere, unaffordable motorways and mega-dams.

How green the BRI will end up is not only up to China but is a responsibility of the host states as well as western powers that would compete with Chinese infrastructural financing. Although the competition between Japanese and Chinese high-speed rail contractors has not yielded benefits to the environment, the USA and the EU seem to have woken up to the comparative edge they hold when compared to China: their environmental credentials. It is no surprise then that the G7 announced a "Clean Green Initiative" and the EU additionally put forward its "Global Gateway" plan in late 2021. By mobilizing financing for western and other contractors, these sources of funding hope not only to rival China's attractive package deals but also to ensure that any infrastructural development financed by it is built on a higher standard of green finance.

In conclusion, what are the necessary changes in the BRI's green credentials to ensure at least a minimal compliance with its stated ambition? For a start, political pledges and guidelines need to filter down to the level of lending decisions. Without the unwavering support of China's policy banks, Chinese SOEs would not be as competitive in developing markets. Second, the political capital that Xi Jinping and the CCP have invested in the BRI is good leverage for organizations concerned with the Initiative's environmental impact. By making sure that Chinese actors are held to their word, the BRI might just turn from an environmental calamity to a vehicle that can promote sustainable development.

5

Is it corrupt by design?

Doing business in China is often associated with informal, "under-the-table" transactions, the vast majority of which constitute corruption by contemporary international standards. A reductive explanation for this phenomenon concentrates on the Chinese cultural concept of *guanxi*, translated as "relationships" or "connections", that allegedly creates an inclination towards informality and exchange of favours and gifts. However, the reasons behind China's struggle with corruption are not cultural but institutional and relate to its economic model, weak commitment to the rule of law and opaque governing system. Instead of a traditional culture that breeds corruption, China has a political, economic and legal system that has for a long time encouraged and sustained a culture of corruption. This reality raises many concerns about business and ethical practices as well as the competition standards that the BRI promotes at a global scale.

These fears seem well-founded as China has been criticized for using bribes to advance the BRI on a few occasions. In 2018, Macau-based Chinese billionaire Ng Lap Seng, a businessman affiliated with the CCP, was found guilty of bribing UN officials to support Macau's bid to house the UN Office for South–South Cooperation. In 2019, Patrick Ho, the head of an NGO backed by the CEFC China Energy Company Limited, a Global Fortune 500 energy and finance conglomerate, was involved in multiple corruption scandals in Africa while promoting the BRI agenda. The CEFC founder and chairman, Ye Jianming, who developed important business and political links in the Czech Republic, has also been detained in China since 2018 on bribery charges. In many Chinese-financed projects, from Malaysia to North Macedonia, Sri Lanka to Uganda and Kenya, there have been accusations and evidence of corruption. These cases play into a widespread perception of the BRI as lacking transparency, consisting of shady deals that are poorly regulated and involve illicit transactions.

Although China's own struggles with corruption are well known, corruption in the BRI is ultimately a matter of regulatory and monitoring efficiency of the institutions involved in its development, Chinese and local. Host government capacity in this regard is an important variable in the success or failure of a project, shaping the local experience of the BRI (Song 2015: 33). There is also a political dimension with important ramifications for China's ability to generate and sustain international support for the BRI. This is not just because its sworn critics jump on any opportunity to present corruption as a concerted effort by the Chinese state to undermine fair competition and gain influence in host countries. There are reasonable concerns also from the Chinese side about the BRI unknowingly providing a credit line to corrupt politicians (Xue 2015: 77). Are these perceptions and accusations justified? Does the BRI promote a model of development that is based on informality and practices that undermine government and business integrity? Is it too tolerant of corruption or even criminogenic (Lo, Siegel & Kwok 2019)? Is it corrupt by design?

This chapter will seek to answer these questions by evaluating the causes and extent of the problem as well as by assessing the Chinese government's policies to regulate the activities of state-owned and private companies that engage in business globally under the Belt and Road banner. The chapter will begin with the evolution and main characteristics of corruption in China and continue with an assessment of the strengths and weaknesses of the state's anti-corruption efforts. We will argue that corruption in China has evolved in ways that raise many concerns about the normative environment in which SOEs conduct their business. The state has been slow to adapt its anti-corruption policies to this evolution but since 2013 extensive institutional innovations have taken place that target the activities of state agents domestically as well as internationally. We will then turn to Belt and Road-related corruption cases and examine whether there is a coherent story on corruption as a characteristic of the BRI, pointing to an endemic problem or even a standardized strategy by Chinese SOEs. The last part will introduce related anti-corruption initiatives, assess their potential and offer some thoughts on how to materialize Xi Jinping's stated goal of "zero tolerance for corruption" and a "clean" BRI (Xi 2019).

STATE CAPITALISM AND CORRUPTION

A key takeaway from this book is that the BRI cannot be understood outside the context of China's state capitalism. Alongside clear policy predecessors (the GWD, the Going Out strategy, etc.), the institutional ecosystem of SOEs, banks and state agencies is firmly rooted in China's experience with development at least since 1979. The characteristics and strengths of this ecosystem are reflected in the BRI's implementation and governance, but so are its weaknesses. Corruption is a clear issue in this regard and has, alongside environmental degradation, weak labour protection and human rights violations, long defined the dark side of China's economic miracle.

So, is the Chinese economic model inherently corrupt? The most popular way to answer this question is by referring to people's perceptions, experience with corruption and law enforcement data. According to Transparency International's Corruption Perception Index, perception of corruption in China has been consistently high since the introduction of the index in 1995, placing the world's second-largest economy below not only all industrialized nations but also many developing economies such as Oman, Namibia and Cuba (Transparency International 2022). It is important to note that the index is partly based on the opinions of experts and business executives, which renders it even more relatable to the Belt and Road.

The World Bank's World Governance Indicators (WGI), which measure "control of corruption", paint a similar story. Based on a dataset that combines opinion and expert surveys that measure perception and experience with corruption as well as views on anti-corruption efficiency, the WGI places China below the average of the East Asian region and upper-middle income countries (World Bank 2020). It is also worth pointing out that the positive effect of almost a decade of Xi Jinping's "anti-corruption struggle" (*fanfubai douzheng* 反腐败斗争) has been minimal in both indices, despite its unprecedented intensity and wide scope. Overall, the perception of corruption in China's business environment is still high, which sustains negative perceptions around the activities of Chinese business actors abroad.

Another way to evaluate the extent of the problem is to assess corruption control through legal enforcement data on investigations, persecutions, etc. The number of cadres investigated between 1997 and 2017, from the 16th to the 19th CCP Congress, is impressive, especially in Xi Jinping's first term when investigations increased more than twofold in comparison to Hu Jintao's second term as part of an intense anti-corruption campaign (Tsimonis 2018: 58). Although at the time of writing there were no aggregated data for the entire period of Xi's second term (2018–22), year-to-year reports indicate that we will witness a significant increase for that period as well. The problem with referring to enforcement data, however, is that there is no real benchmark to evaluate how effective government policies are. Five hundred thousand investigations under Hu was already an imposing number, even more so the 1.5 million investigations under Xi (*ibid.*). All are staggering figures in their own right, but given the opaque nature of corruption and our inability to assess its actual extent, the only clear conclusion we can reach is that the problem persists.

All available information on corruption trends in China, both quantitative and qualitative, shows that corruption has become endemic, despite the government's efforts. But the combination of intensified anti-corruption enforcement and a stubbornly high perception of corruption further indicates that corruption is not static; it changes and becomes harder to intercept and reduce. How has corruption in China evolved over the reform period and what type of challenges does it pose for the BRI?

FROM CADRES TO CAPITALISTS

Before China's opening up, all production units, from village-level small workshops to urban-based light and heavy industries, operated according to central planning directions and their primary goal was to deliver the products to the central and local government. From saucepans to tractors, the rationale of production was to satisfy the demand for goods as defined by the state. In the early 1980s, however, the entire (state) economy made the gradual transition to for-profit production. To become engines of economic growth, Beijing incentivized local governments, allowing them to keep the profits of local enterprises and giving them significant authority over local taxes, fines, levies and fees. These were accompanied with minimum central oversight, which fuelled corruption (Ang 2020: 55).

Chinese economic reformers avoided the shock therapy approaches that characterized Russia's transition to capitalism in the 1990s, and instead implemented a dual track economic system where marketization developed alongside central planning (see Weber 2021). All state enterprises, regardless of their scale and affiliation, belonging to the local or central government or even the PLA, were instructed to become profitable by selling goods to the market after satisfying the state quotas. Between 1985 and 1989 China operated a dual price system to facilitate a controlled and gradual economic transition: (low) prices set by the state used for government procurement and market prices for consumption. These reforms meant that the state retained a significant level of control of the economy, which enabled it to avoid the devastating inflation experienced under shock therapy models.

But the reforms also transformed the position of communist cadres in charge of production under central planning into managers seeking profits in a rapidly marketized context. This transformation merged bureaucratic power with business decision-making as cadres-turned-managers found themselves in charge of the for-profit activities of state-owned enterprises, which created substantial opportunities for illicit personal gains. Managers in SOEs could procure goods at cheap state prices and then sell them at considerably higher prices in the market (Wedeman 2012: 9). Although this practice ended in 1989 with the abolishment of the dual price system, its abuse was characteristic of the privileged position of cadres-turned-managers, who had almost unchecked decision-making power.

In the 1990s, with the dual price system gone and the streamlining of local taxes by the central state, the intensification of economic reform and aggressive privatizations created more opportunities for corruption for local officials and SOE managers. These involved brokering asset transfers from the state to private entrepreneurs and lowering the actual value of assets to buy them themselves at prices lower than their market value (Wedeman 2012: 9). Thus, the 1990s signalled a move from "cash corruption" to "capital corruption", with state assets turned into private capital owned by politically connected individuals, the first generation of Chinese capitalists. In addition, local officials colluded with organized crime and developed entire networks of corruption to sustain their illicit yet profitable activities. A case that combined all these new forms of corruption was the Yuanhua Corporation in Xiamen in the 1990s, which bribed hundreds of officials (including military officers) to maintain a smuggling operation worth $6.4 billion that included fuel, cars and cigarettes.

In the same period, the PLA had become a bastion of corruption as entire army units could maintain businesses whose profits were siphoned in networks of corruption or acted as fronts for illegal activities, including trafficking, smuggling, gambling and others. Still, the state's emphasis on administrative and disciplinary measures prevented China from turning into a kleptocracy like Yeltsin's Russia. New fiscal, accounting and procurement systems and controls were put in place, the army was forced to divest most of its business interests in the late 1990s (the remaining were removed two decades later under Xi), while new laws, regulations and administrative inspections were implemented to capture and deter corruption, which led to the exposure of scandals such as Yuanhua (Ang 2020: 60).

The 2000s have been characterized as China's "Golden Decade" that witnessed phenomenal economic growth of 10–15 per cent on an annual basis and its rapid elevation as a regional superpower with global interests and presence. But the ecosystem in which this growth was facilitated remained prone to corruption as it was dominated by SOEs with links to local and central officials and banks, while the anti-corruption strategies of the CCP followed the "campaign" model that provided weak deterrence. Anti-corruption campaigns in China were "short bursts of intensive enforcement" that served primarily as proof of the CCP's political performance as a governing entity (Manion 2004: 161). They included intensified propaganda, audits and targeted checks on suspicious cases, as well as continuous calls to the public to report corruption and to officials to confess their crimes. Leniency periods were broadly used, incentivizing CCP cadres to admit their guilt in exchange for soft penalties. This tactic allowed the government to periodically report impressive numbers of investigations and convictions to the public, but perception of corruption continued to increase. To many, the underlying logic of anti-corruption in China was not to rid the political system of corruption but to convince the Chinese citizens in the short run that the CCP was genuinely and resolutely fighting it (see discussion by Wedeman 2012: 142–76).

As the main incentives and structures that sustained corruption since the opening up in the early 1980s remained broadly unchanged, the economic boom of the 2000s led to a further intensification of the phenomenon, with real estate and infrastructure standing out as "a hotbed of shady deals and graft" (Ang 2020: 64–5). Explosive urbanization, which involved the demolition of large parts of Chinese cities to open up space for high-rise housing and business districts, is a trademark of this period alongside the mushrooming of new airports, railroads, highways, ports, dams, etc. In fact, local officials were incentivized to prioritize urbanization through a promotion system that valued economic growth more than anything else as an indication of governing competence (Landry 2008).

But this growth came at the price of intensified corruption as officials could use their power and connections with state banks, SOEs and private capitalists to finance and construct massive new projects with few, if any, checks and balances, enriching themselves in the process (*ibid.*). It is against the backdrop of booming growth and intensified corruption that Chinese SOEs, emboldened by the strong political and financial support of local and central governments in the context of the "Going Out" strategy, began to look abroad for business and investment opportunities.

A BELT AND ROAD OF CORRUPTION?

By the time Xi Jinping came to power and launched the BRI as his signature policy, the holy triad of Chinese capitalism consisting of party officials, SOE managers and bankers, and private businesspeople had already "normalized" corrupt practices in economic activities. The anti-corruption efforts of the party were inadequate but under conditions of strong economic growth the effects of corruption were not immediately felt. This was similar to the pre-2008 euphoria in the West that led politicians and the public to turn a blind eye to dishonest activities of Wall Street bankers and investors. However, powerful circles within the CCP that eventually rallied behind Xi Jinping were very apprehensive about mounting corruption and the future of the Chinese economy and the party itself.

Within months of taking power, Xi launched what would become the most lengthy and comprehensive anti-corruption campaign in the CCP since Deng's reforms. This was surprising to many. Although new leaders always initiated campaigns to discipline the party and remove political opponents early in their term in office, Xi's efforts did not lose their vitality after a couple of years, as previous campaigns had. Instead, the anti-corruption apparatus of the party under the command of Wang Qishan, a skilled politician and administrator, gradually and decisively institutionalized these efforts, introducing new laws, regulations and administrative tools, frequent inspection tours and audits of officials and significant organizational innovations in monitoring and enforcement (see Li & Wang 2019; Wang & Yan 2020). Among them, the ambitious new National Supervision Law (enacted in 2018) created a new anti-corruption context that was all-encompassing and centralized. The logic of these efforts was to sever (or at least substantially weaken) the horizontal power relations between local governments and anti-corruption agencies so the former would not be able to interfere in the latter's work as in the past. Through all these efforts, Xi removed opponents and enforced his personal authority in the CCP, enhanced his public image and emerged as China's unquestionable moral leader.

Simultaneously with "house cleaning", Xi Jinping launched the BRI; however, many of the corruption problems that have haunted China since its opening up had stigmatized Chinese investments already before 2013. A 2011 report by Transparency International that measured business executives' awareness of cases of bribery involving companies from various nations, placed those from China and Russia at the bottom of the index (Transparency International 2011). Since then, many cases of bribery involving Chinese companies and local officials have emerged, some of which we will review in this chapter. This has led some scholars to describe the BRI as a process of "mainlandization" of recipient countries that "adopt the Chinese culture and business practice, which may open the floodgate to using guanxi for soliciting business opportunities and corruption to smooth the operation" (Lo, Siegel & Kwok 2019: 6). After all, the argument goes, if the BRI is China's contribution to globalization, we should expect that its impact will be economic as well as normative, exporting China's value system (with its positive and negative elements) abroad (*ibid.*). However, as with the issue of environmental sustainability, the story of the BRI and Chinese investments is more complex than the often-held simplistic view of private and state enterprises from China simply bribing their way into new markets, thereby imitating past and current behaviour of western companies, one could add.

Structural exploitation of the Global South by rich nations originates from the colonial era and then evolved into new, less direct but perhaps equally intense forms, which are collectively explained under the concept of neocolonialism. Neocolonialism, imposed by western governments and corporations, has created weak legal, institutional, political and social environments in certain countries, where corruption has become endemic and part of the routine functioning of government and politics. In such a context, corruption involves both international and local agency, foreign and domestic actors.

As discussed above, Chinese companies originate from a business environment where informal transactions, illicit profits and unfair privileges enjoyed by networks of officials, SOE managers, bankers and businesspeople have long been part of their experience with strong economic growth and weak rule of law. The combination of structural exploitation of many of the recipient countries of Chinese investment and a history of weak business integrity norms, regulations and enforcement in relation to Chinese state and private enterprises creates grounds for reasonable scepticism on fair competition and financial sustainability in many BRI projects. However, to avoid a deterministic logic that leads to self-evident conclusions, we need to identify *patterns of corruption* within the BRI context. Then, we will turn to the anti-corruption initiatives to address corruption in the BRI and assess their potential effectiveness.

THE ANGOLA MODEL

The BRI's corruption problems involve the agency of different actors. For example, certain Chinese agents (companies or individual businesspeople) may actively seek to obtain access to new markets through illicit means, mainly bribing. In other cases, Chinese SOEs engage with untrustworthy local officials and (mainly) state companies that take advantage of the existing financial commitment of Chinese actors and ask for kickbacks at various stages of an investment. In all cases, corruption has led to significant material and reputational losses for individual business ventures but also for the BRI as a whole, highlighting the necessity for more emphasis on business integrity, compliance and robust anti-corruption provisions. But the problem of corruption in the BRI is not simply the agency of Chinese or local actors. There are structural characteristics that render it very vulnerable to dishonest practices, with the first being the mode of financing.

As explained in the first chapter, the BRI has been positively received by so many countries around the world as it offers opportunities for investment in much-needed infrastructure, without the conditionalities imposed by international lenders such as the World Bank or the International Monetary Fund (IMF). Essentially, the BRI provides a framework for lending that does not contain provisions for deep reforms in the recipient country's public administration, banking sector or labour market, nor does it stipulate routine controls over its fiscal and current account balances. This makes Chinese financing very appealing to governments that face serious administrative capacity problems when trying to adhere to the more stringent conditions imposed by other international lenders.

The Angolan case is very characteristic in this regard, as its government turned down the IMF's demands for reforms and enhanced transparency by turning to China for assistance and loans (de Carvalho, Kopiński & Taylor 2021: 6). There is a catch, however. Chinese loans, often designated as "high risk" due to the unstable political and social environment of the recipient countries, are given in exchange for minerals and natural resources. This is the so-called "Angola Model", which took its name from the loans-for-oil arrangement that has characterized Chinese financing in the country since the early 2000s. Under this model, Angola has become the top exporter of crude oil to China in Africa, and China has become its top trading partner (*ibid.*). However, the apprehension about dependence on China and widespread allegations of corruption under the loans-for-oil model have led to reputational damage and a decline in Sino-Angolan relations under President João Lourenço in recent years.

Another example of the problematic nature of the loans-for-oil model is Ecuador, and in particular the construction of the Coca Codo Sinclair dam, the largest hydroelectric facility in the country's history. Officials, geologists and civil society had warned against its construction since the 1980s when the idea was first conceived, over concerns of volcanic activity, earthquakes, droughts and erosion. But the project was revived in the late 2000s due to strong government backing and the availability of Chinese funding. The dam was built by Sinohydro and financed by China Exim with $1.68 billion, which was part of a larger $19 billion package of loans to build infrastructure in the country. The loans were to be repaid in oil and, as a result, China got to keep 80 per cent of the country's oil production to this end (Casey & Kraus 2018).

As mentioned in the previous chapter, the Coca Codo Sinclair dam deal has raised environmental problems, while the feasibility of its power production targets has been dubious at best. But the project was also hit by a major corruption scandal involving a large number of top officials, including, according to the *New York Times*, "a former vice president, a former electricity minister and even the former anti-corruption official monitoring the project, who was caught on tape talking about Chinese bribes" (*ibid.*). Corruption, therefore, may explain the strong local political support that the Coca Codo Sinclair dam enjoyed in the early 2010s, at the expense of the country's oil reserves. This is another case that fuels arguments of malicious intent on behalf of the Chinese side that may have created a debt trap to exploit the country's resources.

Venezuela provides another case of structural corruption under the loans-for-oil model. In 2009 Caracas agreed to repay a loan of $1 billion by delivering 42.96 million tonnes of iron ore to Chinese steel company Wuhan Iron and Steel Corporation at just a quarter of the market price at the time. This substantial discount was justified on the basis of a high risk of default by the Venezuelan state-owned mining company CVG Ferrominera (Segovia 2021). A corruption scandal in Ferrominera, however, brought the whole endeavour to a halt in the mid-2010s, causing frustration for both parties. And this is just one of over $60 billion worth of projects financed under the loans-for-oil arrangement between Venezuela and China over the last decade (Rendon 2018). Other high-profile corruption-ridden projects include the construction of a rice-processing plant in Delta Amacuro and the Joint Chinese-Venezuela Fund, but the list of alleged corruption is longer than that (Ellsworth 2013; Berwick 2019; Rangel *et al.* 2020).

Loans-for-resources deals involving Chinese actors have raised allegations of corruption in various parts of the world. For example, the Democratic Republic of Congo since 2007 has signed various loans with China to improve its infrastructure, allowing Chinese companies to extract cobalt in return. Granting mining rights has raised allegations of corruption, with the most recent one against the governor of Lualaba province in the country's south part, and involving a Chinese company, the Congo Dongfang International Mining (Niarchos 2021). Similarly, in Central Asia, granting oil extraction and gold and silver mining rights to Chinese companies in exchange for loans and infrastructure projects has caused public anger and unrest due to the suspected corruption of local politicians, environmental damage and souring relations between Chinese companies and local communities (DeSisto 2021).

Under the so-called "Angola Model", transactions in "kind" (mainly oil and minerals) to repay loans are very difficult to track and verify, which creates a context for different actors to engage in informal deals and illicit activities (Mihalyi, Adam & Hwang 2020: 11). But even in cases where corruption of Chinese actors has not been established, we observe a familiar pattern where Chinese loans are given with poor provisions for transparency and integrity. For instance, in many cases it is nearly impossible for researchers and journalists to obtain the exact financing terms of these deals. This is a problem that points to the second characteristic of the BRI: its still weak anti-corruption regulatory framework.

WHAT TERMS, WHAT STANDARDS?

There are indications that the use of bribes in order to secure access in African markets by Chinese business actors has become routine. A 2017 report by McKinsey found that 60–87 per cent of Chinese companies in five African countries had resorted to bribing in order to obtain the necessary deals, permissions or licences to conduct their business

(Sun, Jayaram & Kassiri 2017). This also applies to private companies, with Huawei and ZTE allegedly having been involved in corruption scandals in 15 African countries (Meservey 2018).

The extent of bribing is shocking but tells us little about the causal relation leading to corruption. Does the responsibility lie with Chinese or local actors? Are we observing a process of "mainlandization" (Lo, Siegel & Kwok 2019) of recipient countries or of "localization" of Chinese business actors as they arrive in the host countries (Strauss & Armony 2012)? A recent study (Culver 2021) offers a different possible explanation on the causal relation between Chinese investment and corruption. What the author finds is that when Chinese FDI is compared to investment from developed countries, the effect on corruption is very similar, in effect suggesting that Chinese investment does not correlate with higher levels of corruption than investment from developed countries. The difference is that Chinese companies appear to be less risk averse when deciding to invest in countries with high levels of corruption. They will simply go where others will not. These apparently contrasting explanations, one pointing at the agency of Chinese actors and the other on structural corruption in host countries are in fact complementary, connected by the fact that Chinese lending and investment in the BRI is weakly regulated and not transparent.

In fact, the world of sovereign lending suffers from lack of transparency, with both creditors and lenders having incentives to conceal key information on the terms of agreements. The resulting opaqueness has received considerable criticism and there have been reported some "shy" developments in addressing it (Mustapha & Olivares-Caminal 2020). However, Chinese loans continue to stand out as particularly problematic in terms of transparency, which also hinders the evaluation of corruption prevention and anti-corruption enforcement within the BRI.

This disregard for transparency appears to be "by design". As a non-OECD member, China does not participate in the Creditor Reporting System, designed to provide a certain level of transparency on development-oriented financial flows (OECD n.d.(a)). It also does not engage with the OECD's Export Credit Group, a system for coordinating national export credit policies on good governance, including anti-corruption measures that have a direct impact on lending sustainability (OECD n.d.(b)). Further, China is not a permanent member of the Paris Club, a group of major creditor countries that coordinates lending standards as well as debt treatment. The Paris Club commits its members to a "comparability of treatment" clause that seeks to ensure that lending standards and the treatment of debtor countries are broadly aligned (Paris Club n.d.).

By evading "comparable treatment", China has great leverage in negotiating loan deals and outperforming competition, undermining transparency and predictability on the terms of these deals. In fact, a recent study reveals that this is a systematic practice that falls under a broader anti-transparency logic that the Chinese government conveniently believes should apply in South–South cooperation, but not between developed and developing countries (Gelpern, Horn & Trebesch 2021: 11). Despite often defending this stance on the grounds of sovereignty (Meibo & Niu 2021), the Chinese government's clear aversion to transparency breeds corruption and casts a shadow on its FDIs, loans and the BRI as a whole. In effect the practice of "hidden deals" we discussed above in relation to loans-for-oil arrangements applies to traditional sovereign loans as well (Mihalyi, Adam & Hwang 2020: 20).

In the stage of securing a deal, Chinese economic actors benefit from the support of the state and its preference for strictly bilateral, secret loan arrangements as this comes with preferential treatment: Chinese loans will fund Chinese-built projects. But questionable good governance and anti-corruption provisions, and the overall opacity that characterizes most BRI deals in the Global South, create considerable financial and reputational costs for Chinese investments down the line. The case of Sri Lanka is characteristic in that regard.

The Hambantota Port project has attracted considerable criticism and is often presented as a typical example of China's use of "debt traps" to gain political influence in BRI countries. The port is the signature project of Mahinda Rajapaksa, former president (2005–15) and current prime minister (since 2019) of Sri Lanka. Rajapaksa started promoting the idea of the port when he was a local politician from the Hambantota district in the 1970s but managed to bring it to fruition only after he became president. Various feasibility studies had questioned its commercial logic but, under strong lobbying by the China Harbour Engineering Group (CHEG), the project was approved in 2007. The port's construction commenced in 2008 and was concluded in 2010.

CHEG was not the only Chinese SOE interested in the project, with Sinohydro also pursuing the contract. The dynamics of the decision-making stage have been mapped out by a Chatham House study that rebukes the "debt trap" criticism, demonstrating instead that Chinese involvement was business-driven, with the two SOEs lobbying hard to win the contract (Jones & Hameiri 2020: 13–16). Still, however, the Hambantota Port, alongside other developmental projects launched during Rajapaksa's presidency, was ridden with corruption that involved high-ranking officials and members of the president's family (BBC 2016). Rajapaksa lost the 2015 election, partially due to the high perception of corruption surrounding these projects (*ibid.*).

Facing an unsustainable debt, the big majority of which was owed to non-Chinese creditors, the new Sri Lankan government approached, first, Indian and Japanese companies and, eventually, the Chinese government with a proposal to lease the Hambantota Port (*ibid.*: 18). In 2017, China Merchants Port obtained the lease to operate and develop the port's infrastructure for 99 years. Jones and Hameiri (2020) correctly point out that the most often cited criticism of this deal, including allegations of a debt trap resulting in China taking over the port with the intention of using it as a military base (see, e.g., Abi-Habib 2018), are groundless. However, this case is indicative of Chinese SOEs embedding themselves in local networks of corruption and failing to provide pressure or incentives for good governance and transparency. In turn, this not only brings financial losses to the Chinese side by committing funds and effort even more closely to past unprofitable investments, but also allows critics to present Chinese investment as creating "debt traps" by design.

Although Chinese SOEs are often blamed for unfair practices due to their close relation with the state, the weak regulatory framework of Chinese FDI has a negative impact also on projects involving private companies. In Kyrgyzstan, for instance, a Xinjiang-based company, the Tebian Electric Apparatus Stock (TEAS), won a contract to modernize the main power plant of the Kyrgyz capital Bishkek. The $386 million modernization project was funded through a 20-year loan agreement with China Exim. The contract was awarded without a public tender to TEAS, which enjoyed support from key figures within Kyrgyzstan's political elite (Özcan 2021), and despite lower bids from other Chinese companies (Putz 2018).

The result was embarrassing for all actors involved. The modernization of the plant that provides heating to Bishkek progressed slowly and failed to meet the required standards, resulting in decreased output of both electricity and water heat in the middle of winter in 2018, causing widespread public anger (*ibid.*). As it was discovered later, funds were embezzled as part of a corruption scandal that led to the imprisonment of a former prime minister and the mayor of the Kyrgyz capital. This case reveals that, despite the often-held view of Chinese companies acting as pawns in Beijing's grant geo-economic game, China's leaders are in fact not in a position to control the conduct of economic actors on the ground, state or private. The availability of Chinese financing without strong checks and balances against corruption results in private Chinese business actors allying with local politicians to embezzle Chinese funds.

Sri Lanka shows that the broader the scope of cooperation, the greater the danger for corruption to mark the public's perception of the BRI. Kenya offers another example of a comprehensive developmental cooperation with China that went sour due to poor planning and regulation. Under President Mwai Kibaki's "Look East" policy, Kenya sought to diversify its main economic partners by focusing on China and, to a lesser degree, India. As a result, Chinese loans and companies became strongly involved in the development of Kenya's infrastructure, including the expansion of the Mombasa Port, a new port in Lamu and the Mombasa–Nairobi Standard-Gauge Railway (SGR). The latter stands out as it has defined the Kenyan public's perception of the BRI in recent years due to concerns over its performance and allegations of corruption.

In 2011, the SGR contract was awarded to China Road and Bridge Corporation (CRBC) by Kenya Railways without a public tender. The project was mostly financed by China Exim, with two loans worth around $3.2 billion in total, and under the expectation that the profits from the SGR's operation would eventually pay for its construction. The SGR opened in 2017 but it has not been profitable since, raising fears that China could take over the Mombasa Port that serves as a collateral for the SGR, a "detail" of the deal that has only emerged in recent years (Yoeli 2021).

Further, the deal was plagued with scandals from its start, with evidence of corruption in the planning, procurement, land use, construction and operation of the SGR and a string of arrests of high- and low-ranking officials, as well as Chinese and Kenyan employees of the CRBC (Malalo 2018; Solomon 2018; Yoeli 2021). To make matters worse, in 2020 Kenya's Court of Appeals ruled that the SGR contract was in fact illegal, as it was not awarded following a public tender (GCR 2020). Once more, Chinese lenders were keen to provide loans in exchange for guarantees in case of default, but without any legal or business due diligence. By doing so, they undermine the efficiency and reputation of Chinese FDI in Africa.

Economic transactions do not happen in a vacuum, so the operational assumption of Chinese lenders that securing guarantees and collaterals is a sufficient precondition to invest in countries where corruption is endemic is deeply problematic. The absence of conditionalities on structural reforms to improve good governance serves Beijing's propaganda on respecting sovereignty, but in fact it has a wide range of side-effects, as the cases above reveal. In addition, they create a backlash against Chinese lending and more broadly towards the PRC's "influence", as the actual or alleged corrupt activities of individuals and companies become part of domestic politics with material or reputational damage, or both.

In Malaysia, for instance, Chinese involvement to save the corruption-ridden sovereign wealth fund 1Malaysia Development Berhad became a major point of contention in the 2018 election that saw the ruling Barisan Nasional coalition ousted by former Prime Minister Mahathir Mohammad's Pakatan Harapan (PH) coalition. The PH government accused its predecessors of driving the country into a "debt trap" and froze several Chinese-financed projects (Jones & Hameiri 2020: 20). In Kazakhstan, a loan of $313 million by the CDB was approved to build Nur-Sultan's Light Rail Transit (LRT) system. However, as much as $258 million was not spent on the project, instead ending in a shady trail of corruption and embezzlement. After an official investigation, arrests, an overturned verdict and a decade of speculation, the capital's LRT remains unbuilt (Sorbello 2021).

It would be impossible to offer an exhaustive account of all cases of corruption in BRI projects, precisely because the modes of financing used, lack of transparency and a disregard for strong corruption prevention and due diligence undermine any positive impact Chinese FDI could have in terms of improving governance in recipient countries.

The Chinese strategy is to avoid conditionalities through deals that use natural resources and infrastructure projects as collateral and stipulate preferential treatment of Chinese loans in case of default. This rather short-sighted approach may satisfy the preconditions set by the Chinese state for lending, but it undermines the BRI's political and financial sustainability. Research on BRI countries has shown that the combination of public debt and corruption has a negative effect on growth that limits the positive results of the Initiative (Mehmood, Wang & Khan 2019).

In many ways, it is in China's interest to promote transparency, good governance and business integrity in BRI transactions, both in regard to the conduct of Chinese companies and to the conditions it sets for recipient countries. Acknowledging the problem, Xi Jinping pledged in 2019 that the Belt and Road will exhibit "zero tolerance for corruption" (Xi 2019). In the next section we will turn to China's initiatives in this area and assess their potential in changing the BRI's tarnished reputation.

CLEANING UP

BRI corruption has direct repercussions for the CCP and Xi Jinping's leadership. First, domestically, despite controls on information, news on scandals involving Chinese SOEs blatantly contradict the official discourse on the regime's determination to eradicate corruption. Second, although hard to estimate, corruption has a negative economic impact due to inflated costs, "lost" funds and underperforming projects that act as bottomless pits. A recent study by AIDDATA, a research lab at William & Mary's Global Research Institute, estimates that 35 per cent of China's BRI projects are facing implementation challenges, with corruption being a major reason alongside environmental and labour issues (AIDDATA 2021). This, again, feeds into China's public sphere, where voices questioning the channelling of funds to the BRI instead of domestic development have been raised in the past. Third, internationally, it appears that China is losing the battle of the BRI's central narrative and message, with negative attitudes on the rise. With so many corruption scandals surrounding its investments, China is finding it difficult to respond to accusations over "debt traps" and systematic use of dishonest business practices. This reputational damage is accumulating, providing ammunition to critics that is potentially more damaging than the security-oriented "China Threat" scenario. Lastly, as we discussed in Chapter 3, the creation of a new normative order, first regionally and then internationally (Callahan 2016), is one of the perceived goals of the BRI, although we should not assume that it will displace the existing one. In any case, corruption in the BRI undermines China's global leadership ambitions, especially in the sphere of international values and norms.

Not surprisingly then, Xi Jinping has publicly stated that "in pursuing Belt and Road cooperation, everything should be done in a transparent way" (Xi 2019). China's 2018 National Supervision Law stipulates inspections of SOEs and their managers, which has opened the way for a tighter regulation of their international activities, at least in theory. Also, in the last few years, Chinese diplomats abroad have distanced their government from corruption-ridden projects that have been presented as part of the BRI. In August 2020, for instance, the PRC embassy in Myanmar declared that a crime-ridden local project (called the Yatai New City) promoted by an untrustworthy Chinese businessman, had "nothing to do with" the BRI (Tower & Staats 2020).

Until 2019, China's anti-corruption efforts did not explicitly target the Belt and Road, although they increasingly focused on the international dimension of corruption. China launched the operations Fox Hunt and Skynet in 2014 and 2015, respectively, to repatriate stolen funds and fleeing cadres, who amassed wealth by abusing their power in government and SOEs. However, in reality, the operations have also targeted political dissidents (Rotella & Berg 2021). To achieve these repatriations China has engaged more systematically with foreign governments in extradition arrangements, having signed relevant treaties with 169 countries, extradition agreements with 81 countries and financial information exchange agreements with 56 countries (Yang 2021).

This development has had an important by-product, the reduction of death sentences in cases of corruption, a prerequisite by nations that do not apply capital punishment to extradite fugitives to China. Regarding its impact on corruption in BRI projects, at the time of writing there is no data on how many of the more than 8,000 repatriated fugitives were involved in China's investments abroad. However, the enhanced legal and operational capacity of Chinese authorities to repatriate their citizens who are involved in corrupt activities will be part of an anti-corruption mechanism for the BRI that China will very likely have to adopt in the future.

There are also indications of China's willingness to engage more with international and regional anti-corruption instruments. As a signatory of the United Nations Convention Against Corruption, China has cooperated with the United Nations Office on Drugs and Crime (UNODC) on BRI-targeted anti-corruption initiatives, mainly in the sphere of training and compliance. Following Xi's 2019 "Clean BRI" remarks and the ensuing debate about a more regulated and transparent "BRI 2.0", the UNODC signed a MoU with the Chinese National Supervision Commission to strengthen cooperation in anti-corruption also within the BRI framework. China has also pursued cooperation in the sphere of anti-corruption training with regional organizations (for example ASEAN) and with individual countries on a bilateral level.

We have also seen modest institution building, although the outbreak of the Covid-19 pandemic has put relevant initiatives on hold. Through cooperation in training and extraditions, China has established a network of anti-corruption enforcement with national authorities of the BRI-participant countries. This remains a collection of bilateral arrangements but it will be interesting to see whether it will provide the basis for a more formalized agreement on corruption prevention and enforcement in the BRI context.

In this direction, China established the Beijing Initiative for the Clean Silk Road in 2019, a platform for cooperation among BRI members. The initiative calls for greater transparency and stronger supervision of BRI projects by national authorities and closer cooperation "on pursuing fugitives, asset recovery and combating bribery" as well as on anti-corruption education and enforcement (*China Daily* 2019). It also calls for the improvement of local business environments, legal and information exchange systems (*ibid.*). It remains to be seen whether, in the post-pandemic world, China will pursue further institutionalization of these initiatives or keep them in their current semi-formalized state.

Overall, China appears to have finally acknowledged the extent and severity of the problem. However, its "shy" initiatives in controlling corruption in the Belt and Road over the past few years do not appear to widen its continuing narrow focus on sovereignty, which limits transparency and fosters corruption. In fact, none of the measures summarized above deviate from the current situation. By refusing to impose conditionalities on improving governance as a precondition for financing, for instance, China remains competitive in relation to the World Bank but still needs to find other ways to improve transparency, corruption prevention and anti-corruption enforcement. Its ability to do so in the post-pandemic world will determine whether the "Clean BRI" will remain an empty policy slogan.

THE CHALLENGE OF BRI 2.0

In the beginning of this chapter, we raised a few questions that refer to the often-invoked characterization of the BRI as "corrupt by design" by being too tolerant of corruption or even criminogenic. In assessing whether such a perception is justified, the first point we made was the connection between China's economic model of development and corruption as its endemic characteristic. The experience of state capitalism in China has produced immense growth but also significant corruption as it has normalized informal transactions between SOE managers, state bankers, (primarily local) officials and private businesses. As state capitalism was encouraged to produce opportunities for Chinese companies abroad, weaknesses and blind spots in the reform-era business governance model were also "exported" through Chinese financing and investment overseas.

The second point concerns the local political, economic and legal environment of recipient countries. Focusing primarily on the developing world, Chinese SOEs and private companies found themselves operating in contexts with high tolerance of corruption and low anti-corruption efficiency, which is one of the many legacies of colonialism and neocolonialism. Third, Chinese loans and investments do not address either the pathogens of China's domestic development or those present in the recipient countries. The "Angola Model" (or loans-for-oil) of financing, for instance, involves transactions that are very hard to track, while loan and investment agreements remain opaque by design, often under the guise of protecting sovereignty. In addition, as Chinese financing comes with no provisions or preconditions on improving local contexts through structural reforms (which makes it more appealing than other sources) it creates little impetus for addressing the many weaknesses in, for example, procurement processes, transparency regulations, audit and monitoring mechanisms that can prevent corrupt activities. By failing to do so, it is not surprising that so many BRI projects are at risk due to corruption.

Lastly, similarly to China's own experience with economic reform, tolerance of corruption to enable high growth is not sustainable in the long run. China's efforts in addressing corruption in the BRI mirror its domestic policies, which focus on improving enforcement but without strengthening the rule of law, improving transparency, empowering the courts vis-à-vis the government and the police, etc. The rather underwhelming initiatives we have seen in this regard will have to be expanded substantially in the post-pandemic world to justify the BRI 2.0 characterization. If not, corruption will continue to define the public image of the Belt and Road, enabling the criticism of it as a "debt trap", causing reputational as well as material damages for all parties involved and questioning its long-term sustainability.

6

Is it socially responsible?

Corporate Social Responsibility (CSR) has been defined as "a voluntary set of practices by which corporations establish criteria and goals beyond their primary aim of making a profit when planning and enacting their business strategies" (Taylor & Rioux 2018: 172). These practices usually refer to promoting environmental goals, human rights, fair labour standards and the interests of local communities (*ibid.*: 172–3). In theory, CSR goals are integrated into the entire operation process and supply chain, from planning to execution and its aftermath. Codes of conduct, routine monitoring, audits and investigations in response to complaints are the main tools that companies have at their disposal. In practice, however, this reliance on voluntary self-regulation has proven to be inadequate and, as many cases of violations of human and labour rights have demonstrated, even large corporations with strong CSR mechanisms struggle to meet the goals they have set themselves.

At its core, CSR is about branding, creating a positive corporate image for consumers (*ibid.*: 178). When used exclusively as a public relations mechanism, it fuels justified cynicism. In such cases, the logic of profit maximization often drives the exploitation of workers and local communities, overriding any CSR goals. Negative externalities affecting communities and workers can be intentional (e.g., essential to profitability) or unintentional, resulting from inadequate oversight of the business operations, or both, when multiple levels of oversight are involved. Whatever the case, however, they may cause significant reputational and financial damage to individual corporations and projects.

In this chapter, we turn to the issue of the BRI's social responsibility by focusing on two dimensions, human rights and labour, for which the Initiative continues to attract considerable criticism. A key theme of this book is that the BRI is an extension of China's economically successful experience with development. But, as argued throughout, this is not just a "copy-paste" process in which China exports its practices, regulations and standards alongside its investments, what is referred to as a process of "Sinification". Instead, we observe a complex dynamic of negotiation and adaptation in the local contexts of host states under the pressure of global capitalism, transnational institutions and local agendas.

As discussed in relation to the environment and corruption, China's negative global footprint is neither straightforward nor given and depends on the interplay with local conditions. However, as the two following cases reveal, the BRI has substantial regulatory gaps in monitoring and prevention of human and labour rights violations. It is the institutional and structural deficiencies of the BRI, combined with an anaemic commitment to CSR mechanisms by many Chinese companies, that risk damaging its image as a whole. This happens not simply by reproducing China's own domestic problems in these areas but through flaws in the design of the BRI itself.

HUMAN RIGHTS AND THE BRI

Since the 1950s, the Chinese government has developed the principle of non-interference in the domestic affairs of other countries and has made it a core component of its self-perception (it was enshrined in the Chinese constitution in 1982) and discourse on its relations with (primarily) the developing world (Chen 2016: 351). The reality, of course, is that China has interfered in various ways in the affairs of other states, from exporting revolution in the 1960s to actively supporting its economic interests since the 2000s, often applying a "see no evil" approach in cases of regimes with poor human rights records (Osondu-Oti 2016: 53).

In July 2021, China and the Taliban held high-level talks in Tianjin, with the Chinese side expressing its satisfaction with the militant Islamist group's endorsement of the BRI (FIDH 2021b). More recently, in January 2022, China offered security assistance to Kazakhstan during the mass anti-government protests that erupted across the country, demonstrating its willingness to defend authoritarianism (and a close BRI and security partner) also beyond its borders. In April 2022, it chose to back Russia against accusations of horrific massacres, mass torture and rape of civilians during its invasion of Ukraine. Elsewhere in China's neighbourhood, its close relations with Cambodia and Myanmar are well known and recorded in detail elsewhere (Pheakdey 2012; Steinberg 2012).

Non-interference in cases of genocidal regimes with which China cooperates closely, such as Sudan, or those with problematic human rights records, including Angola and Zimbabwe, directly or indirectly enables them to continue their inhumane policies (*ibid.*). "Non-interference" is under debate within China as well, with scholars suggesting that the term needs to be revisited to reflect the country's global power status but also the moral responsibility that comes with it (Chen 2016: 355, 363). However, it remains a key component of the BRI's promise, with Xi Jinping repeating it continuously in official speeches at home and abroad (for instance see Xi 2013, 2022). Non-interference in relation to human rights abuses, in a way similar to non-conditionality involving transparency and good governance provisions, has made Chinese state capital more appealing to regimes with a record of systematic abuse or worse, enabling them to stay in power. Therefore, *indirectly*, due to "non-interference", the BRI undermines efforts to promote human rights globally.

Regarding the *direct impact* of the BRI on human rights, we need to distinguish between the domestic and the global dimension. Domestically, scholars have debated the link between Beijing's developmental priorities and the draconian policies used against Uyghurs, Kazakhs and other Muslim minorities in the province of Xinjiang, to the BRI (Dave & Kobayashi 2018; Smith Finley 2019; Hayes 2020; Frenzel 2021). Xinjiang, China's westernmost province, was historically, geographically, culturally, linguistically and politically more connected to Central Asia than to Han China until the Qing Dynasty's conquest of the region in the eighteenth century. Its location and ethnolinguistic composition have rendered it a natural bridge to Central Asia and, indeed, there is a visible logical connection between China's GWD Strategy and the BRI, which was announced, after all, during Xi's speech in 2013 in Nazarbayev University in the capital of Kazakhstan.

Various articles and reports on human rights violations in Xinjiang have appeared over the last decade that include allegations of serious and systematic violations, citing people who have managed to flee the country.

Human Rights Watch, in a 56-page report titled "China's Crimes Against Humanity Targeting Uyghurs and Other Turkic Muslims" (Human Rights Watch 2021), claims that these alleged violations include "imprisonment or other deprivation of liberty in violation of international law; persecution of an identifiable ethnic or religious group; enforced disappearance; torture; murder; and alleged inhumane acts intentionally causing great suffering or serious injury to mental or physical health, notably forced labor and sexual violence", as well as forced sterilization.

Oppressive policies targeting minorities are not confined to Xinjiang, with Tibetans having experienced similar abuses by the Chinese state's security apparatus, while other segments of China's nascent civil society have also been increasingly targeted and persecuted for peaceful activities under Xi (Amnesty International 2021). It is highly likely that these policies would have still been in place had the Belt and Road not been conceived; that the link between the BRI and human rights abuses in Xinjiang is not causal (Frenzel 2021). The persecution of the Uyghurs (and Tibetans before them) may primarily be the result of the CCP's departure from soft integrationist policies to assimilation into a Han-defined Chinese national identity.

However, China's developmental policies in its western regions and across the border to Central and South Asia (notably the CPEC), reinforce heavy-handed approaches and the logic of securitization of ethnic identity (Zenz & Leibold 2017). After all, Xinjiang is the route for many connectivity projects within the land component of the BRI. Beijing has been apprehensive about the region's border with Afghanistan and possible links to Islamist militancy and has tried to frame its policies against Uyghurs in the 1990s and 2000s as part of the "War on Terror" (Chung 2002), with the PRC government portraying Osama bin Laden as a supporter of the East Turkestan independence movement (Information Office of State Council 2002). The BRI adds one more major incentive for the creation of a highly surveilled and repressive social environment. Ironically though, China's domestic security policies undermine the BRI elsewhere, primarily in Europe and the USA, where even supporters of cooperation with China have become increasingly critical of its human rights record.

Turning to the impact of the BRI on human rights at a global level, the methodological problem of establishing causality reappears. As with the evaluation of Chinese financing in relation to corruption and environmental standards, the causal direction needs to be clarified in order to establish the BRI's actual impact. For instance, a 2021 report on the human rights impact of China's global investments by the Business & Human Rights Resource Centre (BHRRC), a UK-based organization committed to advancing human rights in business, notes that Myanmar, which is a major recipient of Chinese investment, has the highest number of human rights violations linked to Chinese businesses (BHRRC 2021: 4). However, Myanmar is ranked very low across all human rights and freedom indexes, while its government is accused of many violations, including genocide against minority populations (Human Rights Watch 2022).

Where does the responsibility of Chinese businesses and of the BRI as a government-sponsored project begin and end in such a precarious foreign context? The BHRRC report provides illuminating insights but it is one of very few large-scale studies of the BRI's human rights footprint. The authors identified 679 human rights violations between 2013 and 2020 and there are three key takeaways from this report that we need to factor into our analysis. First, there is a recorded correlation between Chinese investments and an increase in human rights violations. Correlation does not equal causation but demonstrates that Chinese companies do not hesitate to conduct their economic activities (fuelled by Chinese capital) in some of the world's most problematic countries. This applies across all sectors examined: metals and mining, construction, fossil fuel and renewable energy, finance and banking, food and agriculture, and textile and apparel, which in turn shows that the problem does not simply lie with the host states' weak commitment to regulation of investment and safeguarding of human rights but also to the investors' inadequate supervision of conditions on the ground and their willingness to turn a blind eye to protect their interests (BHRRC 2021: 5).

Second, Chinese companies exhibited low commitment to transparency and accountability, with only 24 per cent of them having engaged with the BHRRC's invitation to respond to allegations of human rights violations, a percentage that is significantly lower than the response rate of other Asian companies (53 per cent). Chinese business guidelines and codes of conduct, although comprehensive, appear to be weakly enforced and ineffective (*ibid.*).

Third, Chinese financial institutions that provide the capital for Chinese projects in the BRI context were particularly secretive and reluctant to respond to allegations about human rights violations. Only one out of 20 Chinese banks addressed an allegation. The report records factors that created positive outliers, including sector of activity (renewable energy companies had the highest response rate among Chinese businesses – 36 per cent), whether they were publicly listed or not (publicly listed had a response rate of 27 per cent as opposed to 18 per cent for not listed) and type of ownership (with SOEs having a response rate of 27 per cent in comparison to just 16 per cent by private companies) (*ibid.*). Still, Chinese companies overall compared negatively across all categories vis-à-vis companies from other countries.

It could be argued that Chinese actors come from an institutional-political setting that views civil society with suspicion or indifference and do not therefore feel the obligation to engage with such invitations to respond, creating a reporting bias in studies like those cited above. There are also opposing perceptions on whether Chinese businesses perform worse than other foreign and local companies in human rights. It is difficult to generalize and, given the notorious past record of western companies as agents of colonialism and neocolonialism, it is easy to slip into an unproductive and inconclusive discussion. But human rights violations in BRI projects are well established. These violations occur due to contextual (country-specific) factors: weak rule of law, corrupt state agents or arbitrary decision-making. Chinese investors and business actors appear to exhibit a high degree of tolerance and even complicity to such abuses, which has tainted the BRI's image.

The weak supervision of the conduct of Chinese companies at the local level by Chinese banks and state organs and the absence of "good governance" clauses in financial agreements is the main reason behind this situation. For instance, mining is a particularly problematic sector in relation to human rights, involving not only threats to the wellbeing and health safety of miners but also violations of rights and the dislocation of local communities. The BHRRC report notes that 35 per cent of allegations on human rights violations in BRI projects are in the mining sector, including "violence, protests, arbitrary detention, rights of Indigenous Peoples and mining-induced risks for communities in conflict-affected and high-risk areas" (BHRRC 2020: 20). Land grabbing, involving delayed and inadequate compensation, has also been reported in Myanmar (see the Myitkyina Economic Development Zone) and Laos (see Xe La Nong 1 dam), while local protests took place over the destruction of local economic activity (see the Diamer-Bhasha Dam in Pakistan) and cultural heritage (see the Binondo–Intramuros bridge in the Philippines) (FIDH 2020a, 2020b, 2021a).

Without institutional pressure by the Chinese government and banks to engage with local communities and civil society on human rights allegations, it comes as no surprise that Chinese companies routinely fail to do so. The 2020 Responsible Mining Index places two Chinese companies (China Shenhua and Zijin) at the bottom of the ranking as they fail to provide information about their social responsibility policies and respond to criticism about the negative social impact of their operations (RMF 2020; also quoted in BHRRC 2020: 20). Facing no constraints by the funding bodies to promote "good governance" practices and engage in consultations, Chinese companies and local governments can ignore the voices of communities. In Myanmar, for instance, local authorities approved the Kanpiketi business park and the Myitkyina economic zone without consulting the people whose livelihoods from farming and communities were affected (BHRRC 2020).

Although Chinese companies, especially SOEs, have codes of conduct and regulations on relations with local communities, consultation processes and transparency provisions, enforcement remains weak (*ibid.*). Chinese banks could enforce compliance and "punish" non-conforming companies but have demonstrated limited appetite to assume this role. Surprisingly, it is more often Chinese embassies that intervene in cases of contention with local communities, seeking solutions to avoid negative publicity, with a potentially damaging effect on China's image and interests. At the same time, human rights violations – intended or not – often have a negative impact on BRI projects. In the case of the Myitkyina economic zone mentioned above, the concerns of locals over land acquisition and compensation packages have delayed the project and soured the government's relations with the Chinese investor (Thar & Aung 2020).

In a nutshell, the BRI carries the potential of improving people's livelihoods through economic growth and job creation – a desired outcome – but its impact on human rights is neutral at best. Human rights violations are often a local affair but Chinese investors and businesses offer few safeguards to deter local actors from committing them. The above examples paint a picture that is similar to the BRI's negative environmental impact and tolerance of corruption. The Chinese state follows the experience of domestic development, of growth at all costs, to produce rapid results while leaving regulation for a later and undefined stage. Without supervision from development banks and state agencies, irregular engagement and consultation with local communities and a dubious commitment to transparency sustained by weak enforcement of local and Chinese laws, the ways local communities experience the BRI will continue to generate concern.

THE "SINIFICATION" OF INDUSTRIAL RELATIONS?

The "Sinification" of industrial relations is often raised as a negative by-product of China's expanding global economic presence. Labour market deregulation and declining health and safety protections are too often attributed to Chinese ownership, instead of local economic policies, sectoral characteristics and transnational production networks. As the cases we discuss below will demonstrate, Chinese SOEs are apprehensive about non-state-controlled unions, partly mirroring the Chinese state's own attitude towards independent labour organization (Franceschini 2014) and partly their own cost calculations, and have weak prevention mechanisms such as routine monitoring, audits and enforcement of codes of conduct and relevant regulations. However, downward pressures on workers' rights do not simply result from Chinese ownership. Casualization, segmentation and informalization of labour result from neoliberal production models as well as the political and economic priorities and policies of host states. Three studies of industrial relations in Chinese investments across the sectors of transport (Greece), mining (Zambia) and construction (Serbia) will showcase that the "Sinification" thesis (the alleged copy-paste of domestic industrial relations in foreign contexts) does not fully capture the impact of Chinese investment on labour. How the BRI is experienced locally results from multifarious dynamics.

Piraeus is the largest port in Greece and is operated by the Piraeus Port Authority (PPA) SA. Already since the 1990s, successive Greek governments have pursued its gradual privatization, with the PPA first becoming a publicly owned company and later being listed on the Athens stock exchange (Frantzeskaki 2016). According to dockworkers' unions, the decade that preceded COSCO's entry to the port was characterized by the defunding of its operations (minimal investment, hire freeze) to render the privatization a necessary and "inevitable" outcome (DUPP 2011; OMYLE 2015; Frantzeskaki 2016). The financial crisis that hit Greece in 2010 sealed the port's fate as the IMF, the European Commission and the European Central Bank (jointly referred to as the Troika of Greece's creditors), imposed austerity and a programme of privatizations in which the PPA had a prominent place.

COSCO entered Piraeus in two phases, in 2009 and 2016, following two international tenders and with the political backing of the PRC government that approved state funding and provided diplomatic support. In the first phase, in 2009, COSCO acquired control of Piers II (3.2 million TEUs) and III (2.3 million TEUs) operated by Piraeus Container Terminal SA (PCT), COSCO's Greek subsidiary. Economically powerful and politically influential shipowners used their government connections to promote COSCO's entry into Piraeus for their own financial interests (Huliaras & Petropoulos 2014). Then, in 2016, COSCO was the sole contender for the PPA's privatization.

COSCO, which had clearly benefited from the port's partial privatization in 2009, successfully entrenched itself in Piraeus during the Greek crisis, obtaining by 2021 a 67 per cent stake of PPA. Alongside pursuing its own financial and business interests, COSCO's presence in Piraeus served the logic of enhancing connectivity with advanced economies in Europe for Chinese goods, internationalizing the presence and operations of its SOEs and increasing diplomatic influence locally and regionally, all key targets that were later codified in the BRI.

The change of the port's ownership status, rather than the ethnic origin of its new owners, had a direct impact on labour conditions by introducing segmentation among the labour force. The 2009 acquisition deal contained no provisions on employment in the part of the port under COSCO's control (Frantzeskaki 2016), opening the way to transform Piraeus from a workplace of "secure employment to one of heightened precarity" (Neilson 2019: 559). Overnight, dockworkers performing the same tasks in the same port but on different piers fell under two strikingly different labour regimes. PPA dockworkers retained their relatively safe contracts, given that PPA was still publicly owned, but the new workforce that came in to operate Piers II and III consisted of contracted labour. Overnight, 500 permanent posts under collective agreements were replaced by 700 casualized workers, provided to PCT by Greek subcontractors on zero-hour contracts, who often worked in 16-hour shifts, had no collective bargaining agreements and faced poor health and safety conditions (ENEDEP 2016; Frantzeskaki 2016). Greek subcontractors were particularly exploitative and indifferent to safety standards, causing a series of fatal accidents. Dockworkers denounced their employers for withholding pay and failing to provide transport to hospitals in cases of accidents and injuries (Neilson 2019: 570).

Starting in 2014, the poor working conditions in the PCT piers sparked a series of strikes. COSCO avoided direct negotiations with dockworkers on the basis that they were subcontracted, but significant disruption to the operation of the container terminals led subcontractors to concessions with COSCO's encouragement. Improvements in shifts, regular pay, and health and safety regulations were important achievements, but the grassroots creation of ENEDEP union for PCT dockworkers has been the most important legacy of the 2014 strike. Since then, mobilizations have taken place almost annually, with strikes erupting in 2018 and 2021.

The 2016 privatization deal did not fundamentally alter segmentation in the port (Interview with union representative, Piraeus, 14 July 2017). Piers II and III retained a different labour regime to PPA, now also controlled by COSCO, that continued to be based on contracted labour. This created the conditions for the unions operating on both sides of the port to push for a "race to the top", with the aim of bringing PCT dockworkers under the more secure PPA collective bargaining agreement, essentially an effort to revert the segmentation under the 2009 deal. This goal has not been achieved as PCT continues to subcontract dockworkers, but working conditions have improved and cooperation between the different unions has been strengthened, with the PPA union routinely joining mobilizations and strikes of PCT dockworkers.

It has been convincingly argued that the rise of precarity in the port of Piraeus is not the result of its acquisition by a Chinese company but of complex and transnational processes, including the withdrawal of state protection, the rise of logistical governance in maritime transport and institutional arrangements put in place before and during the Greek crisis by the government and its creditors (Neilson 2019: 569). COSCO has, of course, attempted to make the best use of local practices and opportunities for profitability at the expense of labour. At the same time, the PRC government and COSCO have demonstrated a strong political and financial commitment to Chinese presence in Piraeus. When faced with lengthy strikes in 2014, COSCO not only did not leave the port or engage in massive layoffs but continued to pursue the PPA's privatization.

The Chinese embassy in Athens has been actively supporting COSCO's interests, negotiating on its behalf with the Greek government on different occasions (Interview with state official, Athens, 24 July 2017; Interview with union representative, Piraeus, 31 July 2017). But the need for uninterrupted operation of the port and the multifaceted commitment of the Chinese side (economic but also political and diplomatic) may have in fact enabled PPA employees to protect their contracts and contracted workers in PCT to negotiate improvements even in the most precarious part of the port. The case of Piraeus shows the weaknesses of the "Sinification" thesis and the importance of unpacking the interactions between local agency (host governments, civil society, businesses, etc.), sectoral characteristics, transnational dynamics and Chinese state and SOE interests in order to understand the impact of BRI projects on labour.

In her seminal study of Chinese SOEs in Zambia's copper mines, Lee (2017) examines these interactions forensically and concludes that Chinese state capital can open more opportunities for local "counter agency" by host states and organized labour than mobile global private capital, due to its profit "optimization" (distinguished from "maximization") orientation. Chinese state capital arrived in Zambia in a competitive environment to create profits but also to ensure China's access to minerals, build diplomatic support in the African continent to gain international allies, and counter Taiwan's efforts to break diplomatic isolation (*ibid.*: 34–8). This mix of profit- and non-profit-oriented goals (conceptualized as "profit optimization"), explains why Chinese companies maintained their operations also during times when profit margins were low and why they also adopted a more conciliatory attitude towards local demands. The difference between profit "maximization", pursued by the far more mobile private capital, usually associated with companies from advanced economies but also coming from China, and the Chinese state capital's "optimization" also had an effect on labour conditions. Lee's most striking finding is that, over time, the "profit opti-mization" strategy made Chinese SOEs in mining more accommodating to demands by the Zambian state and workers (*ibid.*: 28).

Chinese state capital was very exploitative of local workers, sharing the informalization and subcontracting practices of private capital. After many rounds of negotiations and strikes, however, unions in the Chinese-controlled mines managed to introduce important improvements, including pay rises, more stable jobs and better benefits (*ibid.*: 78–9). On the other hand, private capital was more sensitive to profitability and, although it offered better wages, it was also quick to retrench labour and downsize the workforce as a response to copper price volatility (*ibid.*: 78–80). Lee describes the different impact on labour between Chinese state and global private capital, respectively, as one of "stable exploitation", involving "secure employment but lower wages", in contrast to "flexible exclusion" with "pre-carious employment but higher wages" (*ibid.*: 78), noting that under the former there are more opportunities to pursue pro-labour gains by the host state and unions, as happened in the cases explored.

The argument that the pursuit of "profit-optimization" by Chinese state capital can open opportunities for organized labour captures the case of Zambian miners and, at least to a certain extent, the dockworkers' mobilization and gains in Piraeus, but it does not apply to every sector. Lee examines construction in Zambia and concludes that its extremely casualized labour model, the temporary nature of construction (and of the involvement of Chinese contractors) and the lack of support towards workers by the host state that prioritized completion speed and efficiency all contributed to Chinese companies having a very negative impact on labour conditions in the construction sector (*ibid.*: 83–92). It becomes evident that, with the complexity of local, Chinese, trans-national and sectoral dynamics involved in different cases, there is no one-size-fits-all explanation for Chinese capital's impact on labour. Different configurations of these dynamics create different results. To highlight this complexity, we turn to a recent labour rights abuse scandal that attracted considerable media attention.

The global nature of the BRI means that labour violations and con-flict do not just happen on one site or in one country but are part of transnational networks of labour mobility and exploitation with strong local and sectoral characteristics. In Serbia, China's closest ally in Europe, a recent case involving a much-publicized Chinese investment involved precisely such a transnational scale. Linglong, a tyre manufacturer, decided to open its first European factory in Zrenjanin, a city in Serbia's northern Vojvodina province. The investment, valued at nearly $1 billion, was warmly welcomed by Serbia's ruling elite as a vote of confidence in the country and the company was given 97 hectares of land by the state to incentivize the investment (Martinović 2021). Linglong in turn sponsored Serbia's biggest football league, which now carries its name.

These public relations moves show that both the Chinese investor and the Serbian state were keen for the deal to succeed. Yet after an investigative report by Serbian media, which then triggered an investigation by Serbian NGOs Astra and A11, Linglong's brand has become associated with poor working conditions at the factory's construction site.

How did Linglong's factory turn from a model investment to a byword for exploitation before it was even built? Linglong's factory is currently under construction and around 750 Vietnamese-posted (also called "dispatched") workers live and work at the site. The conditions on the site had been the subject of speculation by local residents, who complained of illegal animal traps being laid by the workers, something that was confirmed by the local hunting association (*Danas*, 8 November 2021). Only a couple of weeks later, workers told investigative journalists they were indeed catching small animals to supplement their diet. Poor living conditions and insufficient and irregular food provision were the core issues over which the workers had already organized two wildcat strikes before their working conditions were even publicized.

Publicity may have increased their leverage over the site managers but also led to increased vigilance by their employers. At least one of the workers was fired and private security appeared at the gates of the complex, preventing further civil society or media access. But the images of filthy bathrooms, paltry food rations and rickety barracks amid the harsh Serbian winter were already in the public eye. The Serbian authorities reacted to societal pressure by insisting this was "the most inspected construction site in the country" (*Novosti*, 24 December 2021) and the prime minister vowed to solve the issue without "politicizing" it (*Danas*,

19 November 2021), as if workers' rights are a technical matter rather than a deeply political problem of Serbian laws being broken during the construction of a high-profile factory.

The events at Linglong attracted national and international interest. The investigations that followed shed light on the practice of using posted labour on construction sites, the particularities of which were not well understood by the public – or indeed by the workers themselves, as it would turn out. The workers' situation was not one of being devoid of mutual contractual obligations or marked solely by coercion. Rather than being "unfree", the conditions faced by posted labour on Europe's BRI frontier exhibited traits typical of exploitative labour regimes, which are especially common in the global construction industry, as also stated by Lee (2017). Here, we can say the BRI merely reproduced the already low norms of labour standards typical of the industry.

The situation of the workers was not just one of informality (i.e. a lack of rules or frameworks governing their employ) but was rather that of organized and multilayered exploitation. Irene Pang distinguishes between "precarity" and "informality" (2018: 549), wherein precarity does not mean the absence of formal rules but rather refers to the insecure and uncertain labour conditions facing workers. By disentangling these two concepts, Pang shows that the construction industries in Beijing and Delhi produce a "formal but precarious" labour regime where precarity is institutionalized in law and company practices. The precarity of the posted BRI labour force could thus reasonably be expected to be a product of the following: construction sector practices, Chinese labour regimes, host-state legislation and enforcement, but also the contracting and hiring practices of temping agencies in countries where the construction workforce is being hired, such as India and Vietnam.

Even when a breach of labour law is discovered, this complex arrangement encourages buck-passing between actors, complicating any formal attribution of responsibility. The temporary nature of construction sites and the rapid mobility of posted labour further mitigate against attempts to tackle exploitative regimes from either the investor or the authorities. In many cases, the construction work finishes long before the reluctant apparatus of a host state such as Serbia can be mobilized. Posted labour on the BRI therefore faces several layers of institutionalized exploitation and purposeful ignorance on the part of those who are tasked with local oversight.

In Serbia's case, the first layer of institutionalization affecting BRI-posted labour is the 2009 "Agreement on Economic and Technical Cooperation in the Area of Infrastructure", which, together with its two annexes, exempts Chinese investors operating under the auspices of the agreement from numerous regulations on public tendering and immigration procedures, among others. Chinese companies are not the only ones enjoying privileged status: some of the agreement's provisions were promptly demanded by contractors from the USA and Azerbaijan (Rogelja 2020: 5). Nevertheless, the Sino-Serbian agreement remains the most comprehensive bilateral agreement of this kind in the country.

More than the letter of the law, it was the spirit of the agreement that cemented a practice of Chinese contractors being essentially left alone to organize their worksites how they liked, provided the projects were finished on time and on budget – which they mostly were. On a few occasions, opposition parties promoted unproven stories of Chinese convicts being forced to work in Serbia but, like elsewhere, these turned out to be rumours that persist despite scant evidence (Yan & Sautman 2013). It was not until a group of Indian labourers went on strike in early 2020 that the attention of the media, trade unions and civil society slowly began to turn towards Chinese construction sites. The first thing that became apparent was that the labour shortage in the Serbian construction sector was being addressed with increased use of posted labour from several developing countries, not just China. Moreover, the contractual arrangements regulating posted labour spanned several jurisdictions in complicated and opaque arrangements: the workers were hired in India by the local agent of a Serbian-owned American company, who then posted them to work for a Serbian subcontractor that was hired by the main Chinese contractor in charge of the "Corridor 11" road between Belgrade and the Montenegrin border (Istinomer 2020). The byzantine nature of the contracting meant there was considerable pressure on the bottom line, as every layer adds another actor wanting to profit from the workers' labour. The contract, which became public during the affair, included a list of penalties that the workers would have to pay if they broke the rules – the highest penalty of €500 was reserved for "organizing illegal strike" [sic] – despite such penalties being unlawful in Serbia (*ibid.*).

The second layer of institutionalized precarity, therefore, has to do with how construction projects are structured: vertical stacks of subcontractors shield the main contractor from the need to employ labour directly but they do not always insulate it from scandal. In Linglong's case, the tyre manufacturer hired two Chinese construction firms, Tianjin Electric Power Company and Sichuan Dinglong Electric Power Engineering, who in turn hired two Vietnamese agencies, with whom the workers signed one-year labour contracts (Matković 2021). Interviews with workers, conducted by A11 and ASTRA researchers, suggest the workers were unaware of their precise contractual status, had their passports taken away by "Chinese managers" and could not provide any documents relating to their immigration status with which they could exercise their rights (Ćurčić 2021). While the workers were happy with their salaries, they were strongly dissatisfied with the accommodation provided for them. This lacked basic amenities such as clean running water, had insufficient heating and suffered from an irregular provision of food (*ibid.*). When some of them wanted to return before the end of the year-long contract, they were informed the labour agency would not cover their flights home. In any case, travel was impossible without their passports, although at least one worker was reportedly stopped at the border trying to reach the Vietnamese embassy in Budapest (*ibid.*).

The precarious status of the workers cannot be attributed simply to the temporary or informal nature of their work. Rather, precarity forms an integral part of the structure of exploitation that brazenly puts in writing contractual relations that are incompatible with local law. Workers are expected to work 26 days per month and are not entitled to the statutory number of days off, all of which contravene Serbia's labour law (*ibid.*). They also faced termination of their employment for "revealing secrets of establishment" or "engaging in trade union activities" (Dragojlo 2021), illustrating the risk they took when organizing wildcat strikes and talking to visiting NGOs in the autumn of 2021.

Measures aimed at preventing union pluralism and free association of workers are not unusual in Chinese construction and industrial sites around the world, as research on Cambodian special economic zones shows (Buckley & Eckerlein 2020; Franceschini 2020). The Indian and Vietnamese workers in Serbia faced an additional language barrier to mobilization that existed between them and the state authorities, the contract issuer, the Chinese site managers and even the NGOs that intervened on their behalf.

Linglong, suffering most of the reputational damage, issued a statement to Serbian media emphasizing that it respects all the relevant laws and that the workers were hired by a contractor, adding they have now had their passports returned to them (*N1*, 18 November 2021). Yet whatever the company's objective responsibility, this situation was possible because of two interrelated failures: the failure of the Serbian state to enforce its own legislation and the failure of the Chinese (sub)contractors to provide a regime within which labour rights are respected. If the Serbian state's wilful ignorance can be explained by the exigencies of rapid development and a likely carelessness towards foreign labour, the Chinese contractor's actions are symptomatic of both sectoral trends (outsourcing, precarization), but also specifically "Chinese" traits such as the suppression of collective action and distrust toward civil society involvement.

THE LONG ROAD TOWARDS RESPONSIBLE DEVELOPMENT

Given the broad range of Chinese, local and transnational dynamics and actors involved in the way a project is experienced on the ground, assessing the BRI's overall social responsibility is not only difficult but can also be misleading. Critics have been quick to accuse Chinese companies as agents of neocolonialism, as unusually exploitative and abusive employers and as indifferent (at best) towards human rights. We have no doubt that this is also how certain local communities have experienced the BRI through the lenses of specific projects gone wrong. Also, we understand that, even when Chinese companies are not directly involved in violations, the "see no evil" approach opens them to justified criticism for negligence and passive complicity. Still, one-size-fits-all conclusions that portray a single-directional causal relation (such as the "Sinification" thesis) fail to appreciate the complexity of the Belt and Road, not to mention the many challenges of neoliberal capitalism for human rights and labour.

How can China improve its global social footprint? Zou (2019) has argued that China's political and legal domestic order creates limits to the extent to which the Chinese state can regulate labour standards of its companies abroad. The author highlights the contradiction of promoting better practices abroad, when domestically freedom of association is not guaranteed, as workers can only join the state-controlled trade unions. However, she also lists areas of improvement, including compulsory regulations for CSR mechanisms in SOEs, the issuing of various guidelines by government departments directing Chinese companies abroad to respect laws, offering employment and maintaining good relations with local communities, as well as progressing on the difficult issue of collective bargaining (*ibid.*: 422). The literature we reviewed suggests that codes of conduct, provisions for inspections and accountability of Chinese companies (especially for SOEs) exist but enforcement remains much too dependent on local contexts, as there is anaemic pressure for compliance by China's development banks.

Still, the aforementioned improvements and the PRC government's realization of the importance of regulating the conduct of companies abroad (captured by Xi's call for a "Clean and Green" BRI) offer some space for optimism that there will be increasing pressure on Chinese business actors to improve their social footprint. For instance, the Asian Infrastructure and Investment Bank has issued various binding guidelines on the environmental and social impact for the projects it finances (AIIB 2016). Relevant developments (especially on enforcement) linked to financing by China's state-controlled development banks is perhaps the top area of interest. The Chinese government can do a lot more to improve oversight and accountability mechanisms and narrow gaps in monitoring. However, even if the most optimistic scenario of a sincere commitment to regulating the conduct of Chinese companies abroad comes into being, whether and how this pressure will be translated into actual benefits for local communities on the ground will most likely be uneven and reliant on dynamics beyond the full control of Chinese state actors.

Conclusion: is there a future for the BRI?

The rise of China was always going to ruffle some feathers. Its unique approach to development combines the export-oriented dynamism of East Asian tigers with a resilient authoritarian system that is challenging the idea that democracy and economic development go hand in hand. When China truly went global and Chinese enterprises, interests and political agents started to explore opportunities across the world, the West's ontological security was understandably shaken and fears abounded about China's unchecked ambition. This book is not about the fears of the West but it did attempt to analyze the ambition of China. We collected questions on the BRI from academics, policymakers, businesspeople and professionals from different industries and organized the book accordingly. By studying the excellent academic work of our many colleagues working around the world on the shifting and multifaceted field of the BRI, we assembled a systematic and systemic overview of how China's ambition is changing the face of the world. But the BRI is as much about China's ambition as it is also an outward expression of its domestic system, good and bad included.

The Initiative relies on the decentralized model of governance that encourages actors to pitch projects for approval by the centre, which in turn maintains discipline through fiscal and party-ideological means. While this creates the flexibility needed to fill the gaps left by the centre's vague goals, it can also result in message drift. It is no surprise that the first few years of the BRI saw the words "belt" and "road" pasted on any international event, investment or project hosted by any Chinese entity. Much like with the CCP's other policies, however, the initial flurry of experimentation was brought under control and a winning formula emerged: underneath the big slogans, the BRI has so far been about getting work for

China's SOEs by using accumulated foreign exchange to offer loans to developing nations. This point seems obvious by now but it is the key identity marker of the BRI, which will remain an exercise in the internationalization of China's state-owned sector, from builders to banks.

There are positive and negative externalities to this formula. On the positive side, the BRI is creating lasting physical and ideational links between China and the host states. On the negative side, the BRI is creating lasting physical and ideational links between China and the host states. As we have shown in the preceding chapters, best and worst practices do not flow in any one direction. More often than not, the interactions between Chinese actors and their host-state partners are shaped by the structural features of China's economy, of the host-state economy and of the global capitalist system and its many entrenched inequalities.

GLOBALIZING THE STATE SECTOR

In this book we have argued that the BRI started life as a scheme to turn some of China's liabilities, such as overcapacities in sectors such as construction and energy and energy security concerns, into an advantage. The BRI's task is to internationalize the state-owned economy, find an outlet other than US Treasury bonds for China's foreign exchange and make some friends along the way. Yet the Initiative made as many enemies as friends. We identified the BRI's geostrategic ambitions (stated, implied and imagined) as the main source of tension with other global players. But when we compared the BRI to the Marshall Plan, it was apparent that the BRI lacked the ideological and institutional framework characteristic of American postwar reconstruction of Europe. The BRI is in comparison a large (perhaps even larger) project, but one that is structurally different, relying on loans rather than grants. The BRI also lacks a clear ideological formula for allocating investments. While the Marshall Plan supported western democracies, the BRI does not discriminate between countries based on their geopolitical orientation – apart from China's red lines such as the One China policy.

The BRI has not yet left a Chinese security alliance in its wake, nor has it spread a consistent worldview. At best, China has used the BRI to reward countries that loyally stick to its foreign policy lines on Taiwan, human rights and sovereignty, but this hardly amounts to a new system of alliances. Yet, although it may not be a grand strategy to supplant liberal values, it has the capacity to damage the liberal international order as it grows. When autocrats in Hungary or Kazakhstan are keen to work closely with China on BRI projects, the signs are certainly bad. But if the BRI shows anything, it is that China is willing to work with pretty much anyone to get some work for its SOEs.

From the beginning, the BRI was a heterodox project. Xi Jinping is the individual most closely associated with the Initiative but the operational and institutional heritage of the Initiative involves the wider economic machinery of the Chinese state. If Xi is the show's director, it is the SOEs that form the cast, a crew of actors that want their time on the stage to count. Backstage, planning bodies, party committees and policy banks try to give the show coherence but, as we have shown, not every actor can be trusted to stick to the party lines. SOEs and private enterprises do not always share the vision of the party leadership and have been reprimanded (or worse) for making investments the CCP views as irrational or embarrassing.

If during the first years of the BRI any foreign investment, from casinos to luxury retail, could be passed off as part of the BRI, the second half of the BRI's first decade has been about quality control. The result is that the BRI has become even more dominated by SOEs working on large infrastructure projects in the developing world. While some coordination exists, many of the projects are put forward by host-state governments and do not always logically connect to projects in other countries. This raises doubts about the BRI being a top-down connectivity plan: while certain key routes in Central Asia, Pakistan and Southeast Asia do correlate closely to China's foreign policy goals, elsewhere it is not as easy to find a correlation between a local project and a Sinocentric vision for Eurasian and African integration.

We have considered many narratives that would give the BRI a unified structure, but still believe our SOE-focused interpretation to be the most accurate. Alternative explanations tend to minimize the agency of host states and maximize the importance of China's geostrategic plan. Such a skewed image then naturally leads observers to focus on the security aspects of the BRI, of which there indeed are many. Chinese interests overseas will need to be protected and will establish a mutual relationship of reliance and support with local actors – from Balochi militants to Central Asian autocracies – that has already complicated China's neighbourhood diplomacy. China's own stated ambitions similarly do not provide a good enough analytical foundation and remain "more myth than reality" (Hillman 2020: 203). While the gap between aspiration and reality is an interesting one and may yet lead to widespread disappointment (Zhou 2015), Xi's vision is not sufficient when trying to understand what exactly is happening under the BRI umbrella.

We recast the question as follows: either the BRI exists to shore up an existing geostrategic plan or the BRI will determine China's future security calculations. While there is some evidence to support both versions of the argument, we find that the BRI does not meet the criteria for being a hegemonic project aimed at subverting the existing normative order, although it is part of a wider trend of rebalancing global power away from the USA and towards China. As such, the BRI will certainly involve a security dimension but it is likely to be a case of security following economics rather than the other way round. It is right to question how the BRI might weaken the liberal international order but we believe security is not the most pressing area of concern. Instead, we turned our attention to how the BRI in some cases weakens the regulations, institutions and practices necessary for an equitable and sustainable global future.

The BRI is an extension of China's state economy. The state sector has shrunk as a relative percentage of GDP throughout China's reform period, yet it performs a crucial political control function for the CCP, because it gives it levers through which it can control the national economy. Those SOEs that were not seen as strategically important have long since been privatized or dissolved, so what remains is the cream of the crop. The state sector therefore exists in a space between political and economic priorities, with targets that are both profit-driven and those that are politically important.

When these companies – logistics giants, energy companies, builders of all manner and bankers to back them all – do business abroad, they take with them the practices and standards developed in China, practices that reflect their privileged position. This is relevant because many BRI projects are located in developing countries where regulatory regimes are less stringent than China's or are unable to significantly socialize

Chinese actors into local practices. In such cases, SOEs tend to follow the path of least resistance and pursue the bottom line over standards: with less political control over their activities than at home, they tend to turn towards what Lee (2017) calls "profit-optimizing" behaviour, which includes some political as well as profit-seeking objectives. Where standards are enforced by host states, however, Chinese companies have had to overcome a steep learning curve precisely because they were used to treating regulation as a political imperative, rather than a part of the business environment in which they must operate as responsible actors. In some cases, adapting to local regulation proved to be too much of a hurdle: missing EIAs, missteps with regulatory frameworks and the over-reliance of SOEs on host-state sponsors to get the paperwork in order have damaged the reputation of the BRI in many of the cases we described. Without a proactive and meaningful engagement with global standards, the BRI is destined to be plagued with poor quality projects.

But there is another source of regulatory pressure that we have picked up on, one that is coming from China itself. As the BRI has attracted criticism, Beijing has responded with increased discipline for the SOEs working abroad. While this might be a welcome development, it may also result in increased political control of SOE activities overseas, something that is sure to stir debate on the role of the CCP in China's investments across the globe. A less invasive approach would be for policy banks to develop and adopt high standards and regulatory frameworks that would allow them to better monitor projects' financial or environmental sustainability, for example. Another would be to involve commercial banks and bond markets to provide more variety into the mode of BRI financing and introduce new ways of risk management and value creation, as suggested by analysts from the Chinese Academy of Social Sciences (Shen & Zhang 2018: 33).

On the question of environmental protection, we have found that the BRI still leaves much to be desired despite reassurances from China about its resolute intention to clean up the Initiative. Partly, the critique is unfair in that large infrastructural greenfield projects are almost always somewhat destructive to the environment, but where the BRI scores badly is in managing risks to the environment in a transparent way. Such risks furthermore stem both from increased access to natural resources and the delay in normative shifts required to protect the environment of tomorrow. Instead of applying China's best standards to their projects abroad, many SOEs sadly prefer to identify the lowest possible levels they can still comfortably get away with. Chinese SOEs have a tendency to rely on local sponsors to provide the required documentation and have viewed environmental standards and a box-ticking exercise in many of the cases we analyzed.

Meaningful compliance to local standards (or adherence to best practices in China proper) will only happen if the enterprises have sufficient reasons to do so. When transparency is in short supply and neither the hosts, financiers nor contractors have internalized environmental protection norms, civil society groups are too often the last and only line of defence. In some cases, their mobilization has stopped even politically favoured projects in their tracks, but to expect relatively weak and atomized civil society groups to police the entirety of the BRI is illusory. Instead, we remain convinced that the most efficient and effective way to "green" the BRI would be through the policy banks that finance it. The co-funding activities of AIIB are a welcome development in this direction, as projects need to adhere to the partner banks' standards and contribute to the spread of best practices into China's banking sphere. Such discipline, we argued, would ensure that BRI lending is sustainable both environmentally as well as financially.

As the BRI enters its second decade, we expect policy banks and the AIIB to remain very much at the heart of the Initiative both as a necessary engine fuelling its debt-driven structure and also as a matter of deep concern for the banks' ultimate owners, the Chinese state. As much as a quarter of all Chinese overseas debt has already "run into trouble" (Kratz, Mingey & D'Alelio 2020), and the decade of BRI lending probably has more surprises in store. The Covid-19 pandemic has made matters worse. China is isolating behind its zero-Covid policy but, across the pandemic firewall, the billions of dollars already spent are turning into new dilemmas: should China renegotiate bad loans or should it use the opportunity to extract geopolitical victories? It would be simpler for China if the loans were all "debt traps" – as hawkish observers claim – but many are just unfeasible projects backed by shaky sovereign guarantees. "Owning" a failed project is not necessarily the geopolitical coup some imagine it to be.

The question of the BRI's sustainability has increasingly come to be determined also by its political sustainability and palatability. Both of our final chapters touch upon the various sources of reputational and financial damage to the BRI from corruption and poor social relations. In our overview of corruption in the Initiative, we found that the BRI is perhaps not inherently corrupt but the opaqueness of its financing, the willingness of Chinese actors to work in high-risk economies, and the structural factors driving corruption have made their mark on the Initiative's track record so far. In particular, we have pointed out that loans-for-oil and sovereign export credit arrangements are highly susceptible to misallocation, malfeasance and, moreover, create a political backlash complicating China's role as a global power. The delayed emergence of controversial details from many of the contracts signed by Chinese actors further adds to the impression that secrecy is a function of an ulterior motive to seize assets or exert control on the politics of the creditor state.

Much like the issue of environmental sustainability, only committed normative reform of key parts of the BRI ecosystem will produce a more transparent initiative. But the CCP remains averse to real oversight, preferring the blunt instrument of disciplining. What works for party discipline in China may not necessarily produce the same results overseas, especially as Chinese companies work in jurisdictions that are not always as developed but are almost always freer than China when it comes to societal input.

Lastly, we attempted to assess the social responsibility of the BRI, concentrating on two dimensions: its impact on human and labour rights. The fact that Xinjiang, one of the most important provinces for China's connectivity with Central Asia, is also the epicentre of a human rights tragedy does not necessarily imply a causal relation with the BRI. After all, China's "War on Terror" and its "de-extremification" policies over the last two decades targeted Tibetans and various Muslim minorities long before the BRI was born. Still, the powerful reality of geography created a strong logic of securitization of the regions connected through the BRI, which may have impacted on human rights violations in Xinjiang.

Looking abroad, we assembled a picture of structural negligence that applies to both the top and the ground level of the BRI. China's principle of non-interference is translated into selective indifference towards cases of human rights abuses and even genocide, as was the case with Omar al-Bashir's Sudan. At the ground level, the many cases of violations demonstrate that Chinese financing and business actors consistently fail to take into consideration the negative social impact of some of their projects. Quite often, human rights violations have nothing or little to do with Chinese actors, as local actors are primarily the perpetrators. But the operational core of the BRI on the ground that consists of banks, SOEs and private companies is mostly indifferent to human rights violations. Either because of the BRI's structural negligence or with the active involvement of Chinese actors, human rights violations continue to tarnish the "win-win" image of the BRI and question its moral foundations. In the end, as the BRI is "open for business" with anyone, China will end up perpetuating some of the most inhumane aspects of global capitalism.

Examining the impact on labour rights is more complex for three main reasons. First, although industrial relations in China are notoriously pro-capital and exploitative, neoliberalism has created a global landscape of deregulation, insecurity and precarity that puts pressure on labour all over the world, not just in China or China-financed projects. The example from Piraeus, for instance, demonstrates that labour segmentation and deregulation under COSCO followed a neoliberal logic that was already transforming ownership status and labour relations in the port. Expecting that an alternative investor would have created a radically better environment for labour in the port is unfounded.

Second, labour conditions at the local level are influenced by indigenous factors and actors. Chinese investments become embedded in local contexts, utilizing their material and human resources, know-how and networks, but also rely on those contexts to operate. An exploitative subcontractor can cause material and reputational damage to the investor without proper oversight and understanding of local labour laws.

Third, Chinese companies form part of transnational flows of labour that amplify risks for exploitation where posted labour is used, for example. The case of Vietnamese workers in Serbia shows how they faced linguistic barriers both towards their Chinese managers as well as from the Serbian authorities, signed contracts they largely did not understand and ended up having their passports held by the subcontractor that employed them via a Vietnamese-posted labour service. The lack of strong regulatory frameworks on the part of the Chinese investors as well as the Serbian state – which only reacted once it was shamed into doing so – illustrate the amplification risks inherent in a transnational network of construction businesses so typical of the BRI.

Therefore, we need to be very careful when distinguishing between the impact of Chinese investments and those of neoliberalism, local factors or a transnational combination of the two, all of which strongly affect the social impact of the BRI. Analyzing this impact alongside problems with corruption and environmental degradation, we find that the BRI is susceptible to reputational damage largely because of a systemic failure to mitigate social, criminal and environmental risks. Because the BRI is an extension of the Chinese state economy, it operates on a logic of opaque checks and balances that rely on intra-party relations, ideological discipline and the occasional rectification campaign. These blunt tools are not suited to an international environment where actors cannot be compelled to toe the party line.

THE RESILIENCE OF THE BRI

The future of the BRI was debated extensively even before the pandemic. Issues of financial sustainability in many projects, the trade war with the USA and souring relations with many advanced economies fuelled scepticism about its profitability, political viability and geographical scope in the long run. The pandemic reinforced this trend as new investments under the BRI declined considerably. In this climate, considerable speculation about the end of the BRI emerged (Wilson 2000; Kynge & Wheatley 2020; Uljevic 2020). At the time of writing, Russia's invasion of Ukraine has sparked a new round of debate on the possible repercussions of Putin's aggression on East–West connectivity, with commentators highlighting its immediate negative impact on freight traffic, investment in Ukraine, Russia and Central Asia and the risks to the BRI as a whole if China challenges western sanctions (Forough 2022; Hutson 2022; Sun 2022). In such a volatile context of an ongoing pandemic and war, predicting the future becomes even more risky analytically (and reputationally) than it normally is, so we will conclude this book by cautiously identifying arguments and trends that rely as little as possible on speculation.

A recent study (Schulhof, van Vuuren & Kirchherr 2021) identified two factors that will potentially determine the future of the BRI: globalization and multilateralism. Both will be severely affected by the Russian invasion of Ukraine in 2022 and the Covid pandemic. Globalization refers here to the continued integration of the global economy in the form of intensified trade and financial flows, as well as the expansion of connectivity, all of which have been impacted by the pandemic (*ibid.*: 4). The second, multilateralism, is the "political side of globalization", and refers to trends in global governance and cooperation (*ibid.*). The authors treat the pandemic as a short-term disturbance of economic globalization, with negative effects such as reshoring and a sudden decrease in movement and investment. In their view, the future of the BRI will not depend on the impact of Covid-19 but on factors that will shape the global economy and politics more broadly.

Will competition or cooperation prevail? Are we heading towards a new type of Cold War (Schindler, DiCarlo & Paudel 2021)? Is the world fragmenting into regional alliances and blocs? The argument of the authors is an important one, as the discussion on the impact of the pandemic on the BRI remains inconclusive, with some analysts highlighting the economic slowdown and declining appetite for overseas investment (Kynge & Wheatley 2020), and others its resilient logic that surpasses narrow and short-term profit considerations (Hong 2021). The BRI's future will depend on the future of globalization in an increasingly polarized world. In that regard, Russia's invasion of Ukraine showcases the fragility of the BRI and its dependence on global geopolitics.

We would add that the future of globalization and the future of multilateralism will also depend on the development of the BRI. With the war in Ukraine bringing about a renewed mission for western military and economic alliances, China's support for Moscow may damage the BRI as potential partners shy away from any toxic association China may have with Putin's invasion and the humanitarian disaster it has caused. This is before we even consider the chilling effect of western sanctions. Alternatively, the crystallization of two competing political and economic blocs may rupture globalization altogether, resulting in a bipolar system more reminiscent of the Cold War.

On the US side, there are strong arguments in favour of cautiously engaging with the BRI, as interdependence may be a more effective way of influencing China's international behaviour than confrontation (Freymann 2020) but hawkish attitudes towards Beijing prevail in the US policy establishment. Either way, the presence and conduct of Chinese actors on the global stage is going to crucially shape how the costs and advantages of changing the current status quo are perceived by all the players involved. An exclusionary BRI that feeds autocracies and scares democracies, either due to a future security component or the reckless behaviour of business and state actors, will trigger a backlash and harm globalization and multilateralism in the long run. For better or worse, China is now also responsible for global peace and prosperity.

Another way to approach the BRI's future is by measuring its importance. Does the BRI continue to deliver the intended results for China and the countries involved? It has been argued that, for the Chinese side, the BRI's value is not simply understood in narrow material terms but also immaterial ones (Hong 2021). The BRI is valuable for the PRC because it provides a platform for engagement with the world in different fields: from investment to cultural and educational exchanges, bilateral cooperation, and, of course, diplomacy (*ibid.*). We do not underestimate the economic impact of the pandemic or material measurements of the BRI more broadly. The total volume of BRI investments experienced a 50 per cent drop between 2019 and 2020, stabilizing in 2021 amid a broader global recovery (Wang 2020, 2021). This followed a downwards trend following the trade war with the USA and a declining political appetite for Chinese capital in many advanced economies.

But perhaps the most interesting development relating to the BRI during the pandemic is how well it functioned as a platform for China's health assistance and cooperation. Public health had been identified as a component of BRI cooperation already before Covid-19 (Tambo *et al.* 2019). From Africa and the Middle East to Central Europe and beyond (Zhu, Shi & Lempert 2021; Zoubir & Tran 2021), the "Health Silk Road", a concept going back to 2015 (Mardell 2020), has provided a platform for closer cooperation in a new field, bringing diplomatic benefits at a time of prevailing negative attitudes towards China. This demonstrates that there is an element of resilience in the BRI as a project of connectivity that cannot be underestimated. Despite economic damage, the pandemic has strengthened the BRI's diplomatic value. Likewise, after the end of the Russian invasion (nowhere in sight at the time of writing), the

BRI may also become a key component of Ukraine's reconstruction, possibly in cooperation with the EU, that is unless the CCP opts to downgrade the Initiative into Putin's life-support mechanism.

Furthermore, we need to consider the political value of the BRI for Xi Jinping as well as the CCP's commitment to its continuation. The BRI will be abandoned only if China's leaders decide to do so. Up to now, although there are calls for more prudent investments and a clearer realization of the risks involved, there is no indication of it being cast aside. There seem to be concerns in Beijing, however, about the continuous appeal of China's development model and assistance. These concerns are evident in attempts to reinvigorate and repackage its economic activities and developmental profile on a global scale. On 21 September 2021, Xi Jinping introduced the term "Global Development Initiative" (GDI, *Quanqiu fazhan changyi* 全球发展倡议) during a speech in the United Nations General Assembly. The GDI focuses on developing nations and on the delivery of growth alongside the UN's sustainable development goals. The BRI's relation to the GDI and the division of labour between the two is still unclear but so far the two initiatives coexist in government rhetoric. Still, even if the GDI gradually replaces the BRI as a term, its introduction reaffirms the BRI's purpose, especially echoing the link between "BRI 2.0" and sustainable development, rather than undermines it.

Perhaps after the end of Xi's political career, the CCP will revisit the BRI but, even then, it will have to be replaced by something very similar. There is simply too much economic and political investment in the BRI and extensive reliance on its material and immaterial benefits for the party to ignore it. In fact its value was reaffirmed in April 2020 when Xi Jinping introduced the concept of dual circulation (*Guonei guoji shuang xunhuan* 国内国际双循环) in the party canon to describe China's new economic priorities and aspirations. Dual circulation has two components: the internal (or domestic) and external (or international) circulation. The internal refers to developing the domestic market's self-reliance and its production capacity to reduce dependency on imports for high-tech products and those of strategic value for China's development (Herrero 2021). The external concentrates on promoting demand for Chinese products and services in foreign markets.

Clearly, dual circulation is partly a response to "decoupling" strategies advocated by many industrialized economies since the second half of the 2010s, and partly a codification of existing economic trends. More importantly, it strengthens the importance of outward-looking economic initiatives, notably the BRI, as an integral component of China's long-term development strategy, rather than negates it. Unless there is an unexpected drastic return to isolationism or to a Mao-era style of radical politics, we should expect either a routinization of the BRI or a rebranding, when a new leader will seek to build their legitimacy by reinventing the wheel.

From the perspective of the countries involved, the BRI has to continue to deliver material benefits while minimizing its costs (political, environmental, regulatory, social). There is a realization in Beijing that the business model of the BRI has to change by improving its corporate practices and negative externalities, the idea behind promoting the "green and clean" dimension of the Initiative. This will depend on China enforcing existing regulations and codes of conduct, disincentivizing corruption, improving its environmental and social footprint and keeping its "win-win" promise. The alternative would be a pariah globalization, in which the negative aspects of Chinese financing identified in the previous pages become the norm. Such a BRI would most likely decline in scope and value.

To conclude, in our view China will not abandon the BRI, even if the term itself fades away. Chinese businesses will continue to look for profitable ventures abroad, Chinese banks will continue financing them (hopefully more prudently) and China-led multilateral institutions will continue to play a role in global governance. The logic of internationalization and connectivity that drives the BRI (achieving energy security and accessing strategic resources, exporting industrial overcapacity, internationalizing the SOEs, attaining diplomatic gains) is intertwined with China's economic model and political desire for recognition. The BRI, under whichever future name, will continue to define how the PRC interacts with the world, offering capital, structure, institutions and, perhaps more importantly, a positive vision for China's role in globalization. The question is whether the world will continue to find this vision an appealing one.

References

Abi-Habib, M. 2018. "How China got Sri Lanka to cough up a port". *New York Times*, 25 June. www.nytimes.com/2018/06/25/world/asia/china-sri-lanka-port.html

AEI 2022. "China Global Investment Tracker". China Global Investment Tracker. www.aei.org/china-global-investment-tracker/

AIDDATA 2021. "Global Chinese Development Finance Dataset, Version 2.0". China. AIDDATA.org. https://china.aiddata.org/

AIIB 2016. "Environmental and Social Framework". Asian Infrastructure and Investment Bank. www.aiib.org/en/policies-strategies/framework-agreements/environmental-social-framework.html

AIIB 2021. "2020 AIIB Annual Report". Asian Infrastructure Investment Bank. www.aiib.org/en/news-events/annual-report/2020/_common/pdf/2020-aiib-annual-report-and-financials.pdf

Amazon Watch 2016. "Which Chinese corporations have their eyes on the Amazon?" 24 February. https://amazonwatch.org/news/2016/0224-which-chinese-corporations-have-their-eyes-on-the-amazon

Amnesty International 2021. "China 2020". www.amnesty.org/en/location/asia-and-the-pacific/east-asia/china/report-china/

Anderlini, J., H. Sender & F. Bokhari 2018. "Pakistan rethinks its role in Xi's Belt and Road plan". *Financial Times*, 9 September. www.ft.com/content/d4a3e7f8-b282-11e8-99ca-68cf89602132

Ang, Y. 2019. "Demystifying Belt and Road: the struggle to define China's 'Project of the Century'". 22 May. www.foreignaffairs.com/articles/china/2019-05-22/demystifying-belt-and-road

Ang, Y. 2020. *China's Gilded Age: The Paradox of Economic Boom and Vast Corruption*. Cambridge: Cambridge University Press.

Arduino, A. 2018. *China's Private Army*. Singapore: Springer Singapore.

Aung, T., T. Fischer & L. Shengji 2020. "Evaluating environmental impact assessment (EIA) in the countries along the Belt and Road Initiatives: system effectiveness and the compatibility with the Chinese EIA". *Environmental Impact Assessment Review* 81 (106361). https://doi.org/10.1016/j.eiar.2019.106361

BBC 2016. "Sri Lanka's Gotabhaya Rajapaksa charged with corruption". BBC News, 31 August. www.bbc.com/news/world-asia-37234654

Becquelin, N. 2004. "Staged development in Xinjiang". *China Quarterly* 178: 358–78. https://doi.org/10.1017/S0305741004000219

Beeson, M. 2018. "Geoeconomics with Chinese characteristics: the BRI and China's evolving Grand Strategy". *Economic and Political Studies* 6(3): 240–56. https://doi.org/10.1080/20954816.2018.1498988

Berwick, A. 2019. "How a Chinese venture made millions while Venezuelans grew hungry". Reuters, 7 May. www.reuters.com/investigates/special-report/venezuela-china-food/

Betts, R. 2000. "Is strategy an illusion?" *International Security* 25(2): 5–50. https://doi.org/10.1162/016228800560444

BHRRC 2021. "'Going out' responsibly: the human rights impact of China's global investments". Business & Human Rights Resource Centre. www.business-humanrights.org/en/from-us/briefings/going-out-responsibly-the-human-rights-impact-of-chinas-global-investments/

Bloomberg 2021. "Bitcoin miners who flocked to Kazakhstan now see 'zero potential'". Bloomberg.com, 9 December. www.bloomberg.com/news/articles/2021-12-09/bitcoin-btc-miners-who-flocked-to-kazakhstan-now-see-zero-potential

Brands, H. 2014. *What Good Is Grand Strategy? Power and Purpose in American Statecraft from Harry S. Truman to George W. Bush*. Ithaca, NY: Cornell University Press.

Bräutigam, D. & K. Gallagher 2014. "Bartering globalization: China's commodity-backed finance in Africa and Latin America". *Global Policy* 5(3): 346.

Brewster, D. 2017. "Silk roads and strings of pearls: the strategic geography of China's new pathways in the Indian Ocean". *Geopolitics* 22(2): 269–91. https://doi.org/10.1080/14650045.2016.1223631

Brown, K. 2017. *China's World: The Foreign Policy of the World's Newest Superpower*. London: I. B. Tauris.

Brown, K. 2018. *The World According to Xi: Everything You Need to Know About the New China*. London: I. B. Tauris.

Brown, K. 2022. *Xi Jinping: A Study in Power*. London: Icon.

Buckley, J. & C. Eckerlein 2020. "Cambodian labour in Chinese-owned enterprises in Sihanoukville: an insight into the living and working conditions of Cambodian labourers in the construction, casino and manufacturing sectors". *Sozialpolitik* 2(2): Forum-2. http://dx.doi.org/10.18753/2297-8224-163

Buckley, P. *et al.* 2007. "The determinants of Chinese outward foreign direct investment". *Journal of International Business Studies* 38(4): 499–518.

Buzan, B. 2010. "China in international society: is 'peaceful rise' possible?" *Chinese Journal of International Politics* 3(1): 5–36. https://doi.org/10.1093/cjip/pop014

Callahan, W. 2016. "China's 'Asia dream': the Belt Road Initiative and the new regional order". *Asian Journal of Comparative Politics* 1(3): 226–43. https://doi.org/10.1177/2057891116647806

Carpio, A. 2021. "China's 'un-Monroe' Doctrine in the South China Sea: Inquirer columnist". *The Straits Times*, 11 February. www.straitstimes.com/asia/east-asia/chinas-un-monroe-doctrine-in-the-south-china-sea-inquirer-columnist

Carvalho, P. de, D. Kopiński & I. Taylor 2021. "A marriage of convenience on the rocks? Revisiting the Sino-Angolan relationship". *Africa Spectrum* 57(1): 5–29. https://doi.org/10.1177/00020397211042384

Casey, N. & C. Krauss 2018. "It doesn't matter if Ecuador can afford this dam. China still gets paid". *New York Times*, 24 December. www.nytimes.com/2018/12/24/world/americas/ecuador-china-dam.html

CCAF n.d. "Cambridge Bitcoin Electricity Consumption Index (CBECI)". Cambridge Bitcoin Electricity Consumption Index (CBECI). https://ccaf.io/cbeci/mining_map

Chen, W., J. Hong & C. Xu 2015. "Pollutants generated by cement production in China, their impacts, and the potential for environmental improvement". *Journal of Cleaner Production* 103(Sep): 61–69. https://doi.org/10.1016/j.jclepro.2014.04.048

Chen, X. 2016. "80% underground water undrinkable in China". China.org.cn. 11 April. www.china.org.cn/environment/2016-04/11/content_38218704.htm

Chen, Y. *et al.* 2018. "Large hydrological processes changes in the transboundary rivers of Central Asia". *Journal of Geophysical Research: Atmospheres* 123(10): 5059–69. https://doi.org/10.1029/2017JD028184

Cheung, P. & J. Tang 2001. "The external relations of China's provinces". In D. Lampton (ed.), *The Making of Chinese Foreign and Security Policy in the Era of Reform*, 91–122. Stanford, CA: Stanford University Press.

China Banking and Insurance Regulatory Commission 2012. "Notice of the CBRC on Issuing the Green Credit Guidelines". www.followingthemoney.org/wp-content/uploads/2017/03/2012.02.24_CBRC_Notice-of-the-CBRC-on-Issuing-the-Green-Credit-Guidelines_E.pdf

China Daily 2019. "Beijing initiative for the clean Silk Road". *China Daily*, 26 April. www.chinadaily.com.cn/a/201904/26/WS5cc301a6a3104842260b8a24.html

Chung, C. 2002. "China's 'War on Terror': September 11 and Uighur Separatism". Foreign Affairs 81(4): 8–12. https://doi.org/10.2307/20033235

Clarke, M. 2007. "China's internal security dilemma and the 'Great Western Development': the dynamics of integration, ethnic nationalism and terrorism in Xinjiang". *Asian Studies Review* 31(3): 323–42. https://doi.org/10.1080/10357820701621350

Clarke, M. 2011. *Xinjiang and China's Rise in Central Asia: A History*. Abingdon: Routledge.

CLC 2018. "Building and Investment and Financing System for the BRI". City of London Corporation. https://news.cityoflondon.gov.uk/city-corporation-and-pboc-research-institute-launch-report-on-financing-belt-and-road/

Clover, C. & S. Ju 2017. "China tells lenders to turn off the taps to Dalian Wanda". *Financial Times*, 17 July. www.ft.com/content/0f240e2e-6abf-11e7-bfeb-33fe0c5b7eaa

Coenen, J. *et al.* 2021. "Environmental governance of China's Belt and Road Initiative". *Environmental Policy and Governance* 31(1): 3–17. https://doi.org/10.1002/eet.1901

Cohen, W. 2001. *East Asia at the Center: Four Thousand Years of Engagement with the World*. New York, NY: Columbia University Press.

Communist Party of China 2013. "CCP Central Commission's decision on several issues concerning comprehensively deepening reform [中共中央关于全面深化改革若干重大问题的决定]". www.gov.cn/zhengce/2020-01/05/content_5466687.htm

Communist Party of China 2019. "The Central Committee of the Communist Party of China issues the regulations on the work of Primary Organizations of the Communist Party of China (trial) [中国共产党国有企业基层组织工作条例（试行）]". www.gov.cn/zhengce/2020-01/05/content_5466687.htm

Corkin, L. 2011. "Redefining foreign policy impulses toward Africa: the roles of the MFA, the MOFCOM and China Exim Bank". *Journal of Current Chinese Affairs* 40(4): 61–90. https://doi.org/10.1177/186810261104000403

Culver, C. 2021. "Chinese investment and corruption in Africa". *Journal of Chinese Economic and Business Studies* 19(2): 119–45. https://doi.org/10.1080/14765284.2021.1925822

Ćurčić, D. 2021. "Living and labor conditions of the Linglong factory construction workers from Vietnam". Belgrade: ASTRA Anti-trafficking action. www.a11initiative.org/wp-content/uploads/2021/12/Report_Ling-Long_ENG.pdf

Dahir, A. 2019. "China's plan to help build Kenya's first coal plant has been stopped – for now". *Quartz*, 27 June. https://qz.com/africa/1653947/kenya-court-stops-china-backed-lamu-coal-plant-project/

Dave, B. & Y. Kobayashi 2018. "China's silk road economic belt initiative in Central Asia: economic and security implications". Asia Europe Journal 16(3): 267–81. https://doi.org/10.1007/s10308-018-0513-x

Davies, M. & N. Matthews 2021. "Water futures along China's Belt and Road Initiative in Central Asia". *International Journal of Water Resources Development* 37(6): 955–75. https://doi.org/10.1080/07900627.2020.1856049

DeSisto, I. 2021. "Competing for cake crumbs: why Chinese mining leads to conflict in Kyrgyzstan but not Tajikistan". CAP Paper 259. www.centralasiaprogram.org/wp-content/uploads/2021/06/cap-paper-259-by-isabelle-desisto-1.pdf

Dialogo Chino 2016. "Brazil mega-dam neglects indigenous rights, says top UN official". *Dialogo Chino*, 29 March. https://dialogochino.net/en/climate-energy/5703-brazil-mega-dam-neglects-indigenous-rights-says-top-un-official/

Dragojlo, S. 2021. "Documents reveal extent of exploitation at Chinese tire site in Serbia". Balkan Insight. 29 November. https://balkaninsight.com/2021/11/29/documents-reveal-extent-of-exploitation-at-chinese-tire-site-in-serbia/

Duggan, N. 2020. "Chinese foreign-policy actors in Africa". In N. Duggan (ed.), *Competition and Compromise Among Chinese Actors in Africa*, 103–48. Singapore: Springer Singapore.

DUPP 2011. "Announcement". DUPP – Dockworkers Union Port of Piraeus. www.dockers.gr/imported/files/anakoinosi_apregia_23.2.11.pdf

Economy, E. 2010. *The River Runs Black: The Environmental Challenge to China's Future*, second edition. Ithaca, NY: Cornell University Press.

Ellsworth, B. 2013. "Venezuela seeks $5 billion China loan for scandal-plagued fund". Reuters, 23 July. www.reuters.com/article/venezuela-china-idINL1N0FT0N520130723

ENEDEP 2016. "Announcement". Union of Employees in the Container Terminals of Piraeus Port. http://enedep2014.blogspot.com/2016/02/17-2-2016.htm

Erickson, A. & G. Collins 2010. "China's oil security pipe dream: the reality and strategic consequences of seaborne imports". *Naval War College Review* 63(2): 89.

Evron, Y. 2019. "The challenge of implementing the Belt and Road Initiative in the Middle East: connectivity projects under conditions of limited political engagement". *China Quarterly* 237: 196–216.

Eyler, B. 2020. "Science shows Chinese dams are devastating the Mekong". *Foreign Policy*, 22 April. https://foreignpolicy.com/2020/04/22/science-shows-chinese-dams-devastating-mekong-river/

Fairbank, J. 1942. "Tributary trade and China's relations with the West". *Journal of Asian Studies* 1(2): 129–49. https://doi.org/10.2307/2049617

Feng, D. & H. Liang 2019. *Belt and Road Initiative: Chinese Version of "Marshall Plan"?* Singapore: World Scientific.

FIDH 2020a. "BRI Watch August 2020". International Federation for Human Rights. www.fidh.org/IMG/pdf/bri_watch_-_issue_1_-_august_2020_-_final-2.pdf

FIDH 2020b. "BRI Watch June 2020". International Federation for Human Rights. www.fidh.org/IMG/pdf/bri_watch_-_issue_0_-_june_2020_-_final-2.pdf

FIDH 2021a. "BRI Watch February 2021". International Federation for Human Rights. www.fidh.org/IMG/pdf/bri_watch_-_issue_2_-_february_2021_-_final-2.pdf

FIDH 2021b. "BRI Watch June 2021". International Federation for Human Rights. www.fidh.org/IMG/pdf/bri_watch_-_issue_3_-_june_2021_-_final.pdf

Foreign Economic Cooperation Office 2017. "Environmental risk management initiative for China's overseas investment [中国对外投资环境风险管理倡议]". Chinese Ministry of Environmental Protection. www.greenfinance.org.cn/upfile/file/2017 0906110647_945969_26309.docx

Forough, M. 2022. "What will Russia's invasion of Ukraine mean for China's Belt and Road?" *The Diplomat*, 18 March. https://thediplomat.com/2022/03/what-will-russias-invasion-of-ukraine-mean-for-chinas-belt-and-road/

Franceschini, I. 2014. "Labour NGOs in China: a real force for political change?" *China Quarterly* 218(Jun): 474–92. https://doi.org/10.1017/S030574101400037X

Franceschini, I. 2020. "As far apart as earth and sky: a survey of Chinese and Cambodian construction workers in Sihanoukville". *Critical Asian Studies* 52(4): 512–29. https://doi.org/10.1080/14672715.2020.1804961

Frantzeskaki, A. 2016. "Collective agreement and labour deregulation: how labour can regain the ground lost". GUE/NGL European Parliament Group Conference on Collective Labor Agreements, March.

Frenzel, F. 2021. "The Belt and Road Initiative: a driver for securitization in China's Xinjiang Uyghur Autonomous Region?" MLU Human Geography Working Paper Series, No. 5 (July). https://public.bibliothek.uni-halle.de/mluhumangeowps/article/view/2406

Freymann, E. 2020. *One Belt One Road: Chinese Power Meets the World*. Cambridge, MA: Harvard University Asia Center.

Gao, C. 2019. "Sino-US competition and the attributes and goals of the 'One Belt, One Road' phase [中美竞争与'一带一路'阶段属性和目标]". *World Economics and Politics* [世界经济与政治] 4: 58–78.

Garlick, J. 2019. "China's principal–agent problem in the Czech Republic: the curious case of CEFC". *Asia Europe Journal* 17(4): 437–51. https://doi.org/10.1007/s10308-019-00565-z

Garlick, J. & R. Havlová 2021. "The dragon dithers: assessing the cautious implementation of China's Belt and Road Initiative in Iran". *Eurasian Geography and Economics* 62(4): 454–80. https://doi.org/10.1080/15387216.2020.1822197

GCR 2020. "Kenya's Court of Appeals finds SGR contract with China Road and Bridge Corporation was illegal". *Global Construction Review*, 29 June. www.globalconstructionreview.com/kenyas-court-appeals-finds-sgr-contract-china-brid/

Gelpern, A., S. Horn & C. Trebesch 2021. "How China lends: a rare look into 100 debt contracts with foreign governments". *SSRN Electronic Journal*, March. https://doi.org/10.2139/ssrn.3840991

Gill, B. & J. Reilly 2007. "The tenuous hold of China Inc. in Africa". *Washington Quarterly* 30(3): 37–52. https://doi.org/10.1162/wash.2007.30.3.37

Global Cement 2021. "Vietnam's four-month cement exports increase by volume and value in 2021". 2 June. www.globalcement.com/news/item/12480-vietnam-s-four-month-cement-exports-increase-by-volume-and-value-in-2021

Global Cement 2022. "Update on China: March 2021". 19 January. www.globalcement.com/news/itemlist/tag/China%20Cement%20Association

Global Development Center 2020. "China's Global Energy Finance". Boston University. www.bu.edu/gdp/

Global Energy Monitor 2022. "Global Coal Project Finance Tracker". https://globalenergymonitor.org/projects/global-coal-public-finance-tracker/

Goble, P. 2019. "Anti-Chinese protests spread across Kazakhstan". *Eurasia Daily Monitor*, 10 September. https://jamestown.org/program/anti-chinese-protests-spread-across-kazakhstan/

Gonzalez-Vicente, R. 2012. "Mapping Chinese mining investment in Latin America: politics or market?" *China Quarterly* 209(Mar): 35–58. https://doi.org/10.1017/S0305741011001470

Goodman, D. 2004. "The campaign to 'open up the West': national, provincial-level and local perspectives". *China Quarterly* 178(Jun): 317–34. https://doi.org/10.1017/S0305741004000190

Gordeyeva, M. & B. Goh 2019. "Shuttered at home, cement plants bloom along China's New Silk Road". Reuters, 30 January. www.reuters.com/article/us-china-silkroad-cement-insight-idUSKCN1PO35T

Government of Pakistan 2019. "Statistical Supplement, Pakistan Economic Survey 2018–19". Islamabad: Economic Adviser's Wing, Finance Division. www.finance.gov.pk/Supplement_2018_19.pdf

Guan, Z. *et al.* 2020. "Are imports of illegal timber in China, India, Japan and South Korea considerable? Based on a historic trade balance analysis method". *International Wood Products Journal* 11(4): 211–25. https://doi.org/10.1080/20426445.2020.1785604

Haqqani, H. 2020. "Pakistan discovers the high cost of Chinese investment". *The Diplomat*, 18 May. https://thediplomat.com/2020/05/pakistan-discovers-the-high-cost-of-chinese-investment/

Harada, I. 2019. "Beijing drops 'Made in China 2025' from Government Report". *Nikkei Asian Review*, 6 March. https://asia.nikkei.com/Politics/China-People-s-Congress/Beijing-drops-Made-in-China-2025-from-government-report

Hayes, A. 2020. "Interwoven 'Destinies': the significance of Xinjiang to the China dream, the Belt and Road Initiative, and the Xi Jinping legacy". *Journal of Contemporary China* 29(121): 31–45. https://doi.org/10.1080/10670564.2019.1621528

Heath, R. & A. Gray 2018. "Beware Chinese Trojan Horses in the Balkans, EU warns". Politico, 27 July. www.politico.eu/article/johannes-hahn-beware-chinese-trojan-horses-in-the-balkans-eu-warns-enlargement-politico-podcast/

Heilmann, S. 2005. "Regulatory innovation by Leninist means: Communist Party supervision in China's financial industry". *China Quarterly* 181(Mar): 1–21. https://doi.org/10.1017/S0305741005000019

Herrero, A. 2021. "What is behind China's dual circulation strategy?" *China Leadership Monitor*. www.prcleader.org/herrero

Hillman, J. 2020. *The Emperor's New Road: China and the Project of the Century*. New Haven, CT: Yale University Press.

Hogan, M. 1987. *The Marshall Plan: America, Britain, and the Reconstruction of Western Europe, 1947–1952*. Cambridge: Cambridge University Press.

Holbig, H. 2004. "The emergence of the campaign to open up the West: ideological formation, central decision-making, and the role of the provinces". *China Quarterly* 178: 335–57. https://doi.org/10.1017/S0305741004000207

Hong, E. & L. Sun 2006. "Dynamics of internationalization and outward investment: Chinese corporations' strategies". *China Quarterly* 187(Sep): 610–34. https://doi.org/10.1017/S0305741006000403

Hong, Z. 2021. "Is China's Belt and Road Initiative slowing down?" *Made in China Journal* 6(1): 15–21. https://doi.org/10.22459/MIC.06.01.2021.01

Hopper, B. & M. Webber 2009. "Migration, modernisation and ethnic estrangement: Uyghur migration to Urumqi, Xinjiang Uyghur Autonomous Region, PRC". *Inner Asia* 11(2): 173–203. https://doi.org/10.1163/000000009793066460

Horowitz, J. & L. Alderman 2017. "Chastised by E.U., a resentful Greece embraces China's cash and interests". *New York Times*, 26 August. www.nytimes.com/2017/08/26/world/europe/greece-china-piraeus-alexis-tsipras.html

Huang, P. 2014. "Three causes of 'Malacca Dilemma' [关于 '马六甲困境' 的三种成因分析]". *Theory Research* [学理论] 33: 11–12.

Huang, Y. 2008. *Capitalism with Chinese Characteristics: Entrepreneurship and the State*. Cambridge: Cambridge University Press.

Hughes, A. 2019. "Understanding and minimizing environmental impacts of the Belt and Road Initiative". *Conservation Biology* 33(4): 883–94. https://doi.org/10.1111/cobi.13317

Hughes, A. *et al.* 2020. "Horizon scan of the Belt and Road Initiative". *Trends in Ecology & Evolution* 35(7): 583–93. https://doi.org/10.1016/j.tree.2020.02.005

Hui, S. & C. Tilt 2018. "Mandatory? Voluntary? A discussion of corporate environmental disclosure requirements in China". *Social and Environmental Accountability Journal* 38(2): 131–44. https://doi.org/10.1080/0969160X.2018.1469423

Huliaras, A. & S. Petropoulos 2014. "Shipowners, ports and diplomats: the political economy of Greece's relations with China". *Asia Europe Journal* 12: 215–30. https://doi.org/10.1007/s10308-013-0367-1

Human Rights Watch 2021. "'Break their lineage, break their roots': China's crimes against humanity targeting Uyghurs and other Turkic Muslims". www.hrw.org/report/2021/04/19/break-their-lineage-break-their-roots/chinas-crimes-against-humanity-targeting#_ftn2

Human Rights Watch 2022. "Myanmar Country Profile". www.hrw.org/asia/myanmar-burma

Hutson, N. 2022. "War in Ukraine is hamstringing China's 'Belt and Road Initiative'". Responsible Statecraft blog, 22 March. https://responsiblestatecraft.org/2022/03/22/beltandroadchinarussia/

IEA 2020. "China: Countries & Regions". International Energy Agency. www.iea.org/countries/china

Information Office of State Council 2002. "'East Turkistan' terrorist forces cannot get away with impunity". China.org.cn. 21 January. www.china.org.cn/english/2002/Jan/25582.htm

Istinomer 2020. "Under what conditions do Indians build Serbian roads? [Pod kojim uslovima Indijci grade srpske puteve?]". 17 January. www.istinomer.rs/analize/pod-kojim-uslovima-indijci-grade-srpske-puteve/%20

ITC 2020. "Trade Map – List of Exporters for the Selected Product". ITC. www.trademap.org/Country_SelProduct_TS.aspx?nvpm=1%7c%7c%7c%7c%7c%7cTOTAL%7c%7c%7c2%7c1%7c2%7c2%7c1%7c2%7c1%7c%7c1

Jackson, S. 2016. "Does China have a Monroe Doctrine? Evidence for regional exclusion". *Strategic Studies Quarterly* 10(4): 64–89.

Jakobson, L. & D. Knox. 2010. *New Foreign Policy Actors in China*. SIPRI. www.sipri.org/publications/2010/sipri-policy-papers/new-foreign-policy-actors-china

Jiang, S. *et al.* 2021. "Policy assessments for the carbon emission flows and sustainability of Bitcoin blockchain operation in China". *Nature Communications* 12(1): 1938. https://doi.org/10.1038/s41467-021-22256-3

Jiang, Y. 2008. "Australia–China FTA: China's domestic politics and the roots of different national approaches to FTAs". *Australian Journal of International Affairs* 62(2): 179–95. https://doi.org/10.1080/10357710802060543

Johnston, A. 2003. "Is China a status quo power?" *International Security* 27(4): 5–56. https://doi.org/10.1162/016228803321951081

Jones, L. & S. Hameiri 2020. "Debunking the myth of 'debt-trap diplomacy'". *Chatham House* 44. www.chathamhouse.org/sites/default/files/2020-08-25-debunking-myth-debt-trap-diplomacy-jones-hameiri.pdf

Jones, L. & J. Zeng 2019. "Understanding China's 'Belt and Road Initiative': beyond 'Grand Strategy' to a state transformation analysis". *Third World Quarterly* 40(8): 1415–39. https://doi.org/10.1080/01436597.2018.1559046

Jones, L. & Y. Zou 2017. "Rethinking the role of state-owned enterprises in China's rise". *New Political Economy* 22(6): 743–60. https://doi.org/10.1080/13563467.2017.1321625

Kardon, I. 2020. "China's Development of Expeditionary Capabilities: 'Bases and Access Points'". Testimony before the US–China Economic and Security Review Commission, February 20. www.uscc.gov/sites/default/files/Kardon_Written%20Testimony.pdf

Kennedy, P. 1991. *Grand Strategies in War and Peace*. New Haven, CT: Yale University Press.

Kernen, A. & K. Lam 2014. "Workforce localization among Chinese state-owned enterprises (SOEs) in Ghana". In S. Zhao (ed.), *China in Africa: Strategic Motives and Economic Interests*, 158–77. Abingdon: Routledge.

Khatchadourian, R. 2008. "The stolen forests". *The New Yorker*, 29 September. www.newyorker.com/magazine/2008/10/06/the-stolen-forests

Kilby, C. 2009. "The political economy of conditionality: an empirical analysis of World Bank loan disbursements". *Journal of Development Economics* 89(1): 51–61. https://doi.org/10.1016/j.jdeveco.2008.06.014

Klinger, J. & J. Muldavin 2019. "New geographies of development: grounding China's global integration". *Territory, Politics, Governance* 7(1): 1–21. https://doi.org/10.1080/21622671.2018.1559757

Knoerich, J. & F. Urdinez 2019. "Contesting contested multilateralism: why the West joined the rest in founding the Asian Infrastructure Investment Bank". *Chinese Journal of International Politics* 12(3): 333–70. https://doi.org/10.1093/cjip/poz007

Kratz, A., M. Mingey & D. D'Alelio 2020. "Seeking relief: China's overseas debt after COVID-19". Rhodium Group. 8 October. https://rhg.com/research/seeking-relief/

Kroeber, A. 2016. *China's Economy: What Everyone Needs to Know*. New York , NY: Oxford University Press.

Kunz, D. 1997. "The Marshall Plan reconsidered: a complex of motives". *Foreign Affairs* 76(3): 162. https://doi.org/10.2307/20048105

Kynge, J. & J. Wheatley 2020. "China pulls back from the world: rethinking Xi's 'Project of the Century'". *Financial Times*, 11 December. www.ft.com/content/d9bd8059-d05c-4e6f-968b-1672241ec1f6

Landry, P. 2008. *Decentralized Authoritarianism in China: The Communist Party's Control of Local Elites in the Post-Mao Era*. Cambridge: Cambridge University Press.

Laurance, W. *et al.* 2011. "The fate of Amazonian forest fragments: a 32-year investigation". *Biological Conservation* 144(1): 56–67. https://doi.org/10.1016/j.biocon.2010.09.021

Lechner, A., F. Chan & A. Campos-Arceiz 2018. "Biodiversity conservation should be a core value of China's Belt and Road Initiative". *Nature Ecology & Evolution* 2(3): 408–409. https://doi.org/10.1038/s41559-017-0452-8

Lee, C. 2017. *The Spectre of Global China: Politics, Labor and Foreign Investment in Africa*. Chicago, IL: University of Chicago Press.

Li, L. & P. Wang 2019. "From institutional interaction to institutional integration: the National Supervisory Commission and China's new anti-corruption model". *China Quarterly* 240(Dec): 967–89. https://doi.org/10.1017/S0305741019000596

Li, M. 2019. "China's economic power in Asia: the Belt and Road Initiative and the Local Guangxi government's role". Asian Perspective 43(2): 273–95. https://doi.org/10.1353/apr.2019.0011

Li, Z., K. Gallagher & D. Mauzerall 2020. "China's global power: estimating Chinese foreign direct investment in the electric power sector". *Energy Policy* 136(Jan): 111056. https://doi.org/10.1016/j.enpol.2019.111056

Li, Z. *et al.* 2020. "Agricultural water demands in Central Asia under 1.5° C and 2.0° C global warming". *Agricultural Water Management* 231(Mar): 106020. https://doi.org/10.1016/j.agwat.2020.106020

Lin, L.-W. & C. Milhaupt 2013. "We are the (national) champions: understanding the mechanisms of state capitalism in China". *Stanford Law School* 65: 697.

Lin, S., J. Sidaway & C. Woon 2019. "Reordering China, respacing the world: Belt and Road Initiative (一带一路) as an emergent geopolitical culture". *Professional Geographer* 71(3): 507–22. https://doi.org/10.1080/00330124.2018.1547979

Liou, C. 2009. "Bureaucratic politics and overseas investment by Chinese state-owned oil companies: illusory champions". *Asian Survey* 49(4): 670–90. https://doi.org/10.1525/as.2009.49.4.670

Liu, J., S. Zhang & F. Wagner 2018. "Exploring the driving forces of energy consumption and environmental pollution in China's cement industry at the provincial level". *Journal of Cleaner Production* 184(May): 274–85. https://doi.org/10.1016/j.jclepro.2018.02.277

Liu, L., B. Bao & J. Ou 2006. "Interpreting the 'Malacca Dilemma': on the strategy of China's petroleum transportation safety [解读 '马六甲困局'-试论中国石油运输安全战略]". *Journal of Brokerage* [经纪人学报] 1.

Liu, X. *et al.* 2019. "Risks of biological invasion on the Belt and Road". *Current Biology* 29(3): 499–505. https://doi.org/10.1016/j.cub.2018.12.036

Lo, T., D. Siegel & S. Kwok (eds) 2019. *Organized Crime and Corruption Across Borders: Exploring the Belt and Road Initiative*. Abingdon: Routledge.

Losos, E. *et al.* 2019. "Reducing environmental risks from Belt and Road Initiative investments in transportation infrastructure". SSRN Scholarly Paper 3323121. https://papers.ssrn.com/abstract=3323121

Ma, T. *et al.* 2020. "China's improving inland surface water quality since 2003". *Science Advances* 6(1). https://doi.org/10.1126/sciadv.aau3798

Maçães, B. 2018. *Belt and Road: A Chinese World Order*. London: Hurst.

Malalo, H. 2018. "Kenya arrests two top officials for suspected corruption over new $3 billion railway". Reuters, 11 August. www.reuters.com/article/us-kenya-corruption-railway-idUSKBN1KW07L

Manuel, R. 2019. "Twists in the Belt and Road". *China Leadership Monitor*, 1 September. www.prcleader.org/manuel-belt-road

Manion, M. 2004. *Corruption By Design: Building Clean Government in Mainland China and Hong Kong*. Cambridge, MA: Harvard University Press.

Mardell, J. 2020. "China's 'Health Silk Road': adapting the BRI to a pandemic-era world". Mercator Institute for China Studies. https://merics.org/en/short-analysis/chinas-health-silk-road-adapting-bri-pandemic-era-world

Markusen, M. 2022. "The quiet expansion of Chinese private security companies". Center for Strategic and International Studies. https://csis-website-prod.s3.amazonaws.com/s3fs-public/publication/220112_Markusen_StealthIndustry_ChinesePSCs.pdf?agENkxBjcx0dJsycSrvu_Y_AmBObnHNk

Martinović, I. 2021. "The struggle of Vietnamese workers for better conditions in Serbia. What is known? [Borba vijetnamskih radnika za bolje uslove u Srbiji. Šta se zna?]". Radio Free Europe [Radio Slobodna Evropa], 18 November. www.slobodnaevropa.org/a/radnici-linglong-zrenjanin-protest/31567923.html

Marton, A., T. McGee & D. Paterson 1995. "Northeast Asian economic cooperation and the Tumen River Area Development Project". *Pacific Affairs* 68(1): 8. https://doi.org/10.2307/2759766

Matković, A. 2021. "Unfree labor, from Hanoi to Belgrade: Chinese investment and labor dispatch in the case of 750 workers from Vietnam". Institute of Economic Sciences, Belgrade: *Significance of Institutional Changes in the Serbian Economy Through History* [Značaj Institucionalnih Promena u Ekonomiji Srbije Kroz Istoriju] (Dec): 114–34.

Matthews, N. & S. Motta 2015. "Chinese state-owned enterprise investment in Mekong Hydropower: political and economic drivers and their implications across the water, energy, food nexus". *Water* 7(11): 6269–84. https://doi.org/10.3390/w7116269

Mearsheimer, J. 2001. *The Tragedy of Great Power Politics*. New York, NY: Norton.

Mehmood, F., B. Wang & H. Khan 2019. "Does public debt stifle economic growth and increase income inequality in Belt & Road countries? The role of corruption". *European*

Journal of Business and Management 11(3): 142–57. https://doi.org/10.7176/EJBM/11-33-15

Mei, X. 2016. "Gwadar Port and China's energy imports [瓜达尔港与中国能源进口]". 20 December. http://magazine.caijing.com.cn/20161220/4214477.shtml

Meibo, H. & D. Niu 2021. "How China lends: truth and reality". *Global Times*, 25 July. www.globaltimes.cn/page/202107/1229605.shtml

Men, H. 2018. "Strategic thinking on the rule-making power of the 'Belt and Road' ['一带一路' 规则制定权的战略思考]". *World Economics and Politics* [世界经济与政治] 7: 19–40.

Mendis, P. & J. Wang 2020. "Why China is trying to copy Japan's old political plan for declaring primacy in Asia". *The National Interest*, 5 September 2020. https://nationalinterest.org/feature/why-china-trying-copy-japan%E2%80%99s-old-political-plan-declaring-primacy-asia-168367

Meservey, J. 2018. "Chinese corruption in Africa undermines Beijing's rhetoric about friendship with the continent". The Heritage Foundation. www.heritage.org/global-politics/report/chinese-corruption-africa-undermines-beijings-rhetoric-about-friendship-the

Mihalyi, D., A. Adam & J. Hwang 2020. "Resource-backed loans: pitfalls and potential". *Natural Resource Governance Institute*, February, 48.

Miller, A. 2008. "China's new party leadership". *China Leadership Monitor* 23(1): 1–10.

Millward, J. 2007. *Eurasian Crossroads: A History of Xinjiang*. New York, NY: Columbia University Press.

Mingey, M. & A. Kratz 2021. "China's Belt and Road: down but not out". Rhodium Group, 4 January. https://rhg.com/research/bri-down-out/

Mirski, S. 2014. "The false promise of Chinese integration into the liberal international order". *The National Interest*, 3 December. https://nationalinterest.org/feature/the-false-promise-chinese-integration-the-liberal-11776

Mitzen, J. 2015. "Illusion or intention? Talking grand strategy into existence". *Security Studies* 24(1): 61–94. https://doi.org/10.1080/09636412.2015.1003724

Montinola, G., Y. Qian & B. Weingast 1995. "Federalism, Chinese style: the political basis for economic success in China". *World Politics* 48(1): 50–81. https://doi.org/10.1353/wp.1995.0003

Mustapha, S. & R. Olivares-Caminal 2020. "Improving transparency of lending to sovereign governments". ODI working paper 583(Jul): 24.

N1 2021. "Linglong: Vietnamese workers hired by subcontractor have passports returned [Linglong: Vijetnamce angažovao izvođač radova, vraćeni su im pasoši]". N1, 18 November. https://rs.n1info.com/biznis/linglong-vijetnamce-angazovao-izvodjac-radova-vraceni-su-im-pasosi/

Narins, T. & J. Agnew 2019. "Missing from the map: Chinese exceptionalism, sovereignty regimes and the Belt Road Initiative". *Geopolitics* 25(4): 809–37. https://doi.org/10.1080/14650045.2019.1601082

National Bureau of Statistics of China 2020. "Statistical Communiqué of the People's Republic of China on the 2019 National Economic and Social Development". 28 February. www.stats.gov.cn/english/PressRelease/202002/t20200228_1728917.html

Naughton, B. & K. Tsai (eds) 2015. *State Capitalism, Institutional Adaptation, and the Chinese Miracle*. Cambridge: Cambridge University Press.

Neilson, B. 2019. "Precarious in Piraeus: on the making of labour insecurity in a port concession". *Globalizations* 16(4): 559–74. https://doi.org/10.1080/14747731.2018.1463755

Ng, E. 2018. "Botched Chinese railway projects in Africa is a warning to Belt and Road investors". *South China Morning Post*, 29 October. www.scmp.com/business/banking-finance/article/2170549/botched-chinese-railway-project-africa-warning-belt-and

Niarchos, N. 2021. "The dark side of Congo's cobalt rush". *The New Yorker*, 24 May. www. newyorker.com/magazine/2021/05/31/the-dark-side-of-congos-cobalt-rush

Nugent, C. & C. Campell 2021. "The U.S. and China are battling for influence in Latin America, and the pandemic has raised the stakes". *Time*, 4 February. https://time.com/ 5936037/us-china-latin-america-influence/

Oakes, T. 2004. "Building a southern dynamo: Guizhou and state power". *China Quarterly* 178(Jun): 467–87. https://doi.org/10.1017/S0305741004000268

OECD 2018. "China's Belt and Road Initiative in the global trade, investment and finance landscape". OECD Business and Finance Outlook. www.oecd.org/finance/Chinas-Belt-and-Road-Initiative-in-the-global-trade-investment-and-finance-landscape.pdf

OECD n.d.(a). "Development Finance Standards". OECD. www.oecd.org/dac/ financing-sustainable-development/development-finance-standards/#resources

OECD n.d.(b). "Export credits". www.oecd.org/trade/topics/export-credits/

OMYLE 2015. "Announcement". OMYLE – Federation of Greek Port Workers. https:// e-limania.blogspot.com/2015/10/19102015_22.html

Organski, A. 1958. *World Politics*. New York, NY: Knopf.

Osondu-Oti, A. 2016. "China and Africa: human rights perspective". *Africa Development (Afrique et Développement)* 41(1): 49–80.

Özcan, G. 2021. "Chinese business in Central Asia: how crony capitalism is eroding justice". Foreign Policy Research Institute, Central Asia Papers (Mar). www.fpri.org/article/ 2021/03/chinese-business-in-central-asia-how-crony-capitalism-is-eroding-justice/

Paik, K.-W. 2021. "Russian energy firms in the eastern market". In E. Buchanan (ed.), *Russian Energy Strategy in the Asia-Pacific: Implications for Australia*, 105–39. Acton, ACT: Australian National University Press.

Pang, I. 2019. "The legal construction of precarity: lessons from the construction sectors in Beijing and Delhi". *Critical Sociology* 45(4/5): 549–64. https://doi.org/10.1177/ 0896920518792615

Pantucci, R. 2019. "The dragon's cuddle: China's security power projection into Central Asia and lessons for the Belt and Road Initiative". In N. Rolland (ed.), *Securing the Belt and Road Initiative: China's Evolving Military Engagement along the Silk Roads*, 59–70. NBR Special Report 80. www.nbr.org/publication/securing-the-belt-and-road-initiative-chinas-evolving-military-engagement-along-the-silk-roads/

Paris Club n.d. "What does comparability of treatment mean?" https://clubdeparis.org/ en/communications/page/what-does-comparability-of-treatment-mean

Pavlićević, D. & A. Kratz 2017. "Implications of Sino-Japanese rivalry in high-speed railways for Southeast Asia". *East Asian Policy* 9(2): 15–25.

Pearson, M. 2015. "State-owned business and party–state regulation in China's modern political economy". In B. Naughton & K. Tsai (eds), *State Capitalism, Institutional Adaptation and the Chinese Miracle*, 27–45. Cambridge: Cambridge University Press.

Pehrson, C. 2006. "String of pearls: meeting the challenge of China's rising power across the Asian littoral". Carlisle Papers in Security Strategy. Fort Belvoir, VA: Defense Technical Information Center. https://doi.org/10.21236/ADA451318

Pelagidis, T. 2019. "China's backdoor to Europe". Brookings Institution. www.brookings. edu/blog/up-front/2019/04/15/chinas-backdoor-to-europe/

People's Map of Global China 2021. https://thepeoplesmap.net/project/central-asia-china-gas-pipeline-line-a-line-b-and-line-c/

Peterson, C. 2020. "Guns-for-hire: Chinese mercenaries on the 21st century Silk Road". *Washington International Law Journal* 30(1): 116–43.

Pheakdey, H. 2012. "Cambodia–China relations: a positive-sum game?" *Journal of Current Southeast Asian Affairs* 31(2): 57–85. https://doi.org/10.1177/186810341203100203

Putz, C. 2018. "Bitter cold hits Bishkek, Chinese-repaired power plant breaks down". *The Diplomat*, 30 January. https://thediplomat.com/2018/01/bitter-cold-hits-bishkek-chinese-repaired-power-plant-breaks-down/

Rabe, W. & G. Kostka 2021. "Leaping over the Dragon's Gate: the 'Air Silk Road' between Henan Province and Luxembourg". *China Quarterly*, December, 1–23. https://doi.org/10.1017/S0305741021001120

Radio Free Europe 2021. "Anti-China protests staged across Kazakhstan; at least 20 detained". Radio Free Europe/Radio Liberty, 27 March. www.rferl.org/a/kazakhstan-china-influence-protests/31172596.html

Rajagopalan, R. 2018. "A new China military base in Pakistan?" *The Diplomat*, 9 February. https://thediplomat.com/2018/02/a-new-china-military-base-in-pakistan/

Rangel, C. *et al.* 2020. "The China deals. Agreements that have undermined Venezuelan democracy". Transparencia Venezuela. https://transparencia.org.ve/wp-content/uploads/2020/09/The-China-Deals-Transparencia-Venezuela-august-2020.pdf

Rehman, A. & B. Walker 2020. "Pakistani military in charge, provinces sidelined in a revived CPEC". *The Third Pole*, 5 October. www.thethirdpole.net/en/energy/pakistani-military-in-charge-provinces-sidelined-in-a-revived-cpec/

Ren, X. 2016. "China as an institution-builder: the case of the AIIB". *Pacific Review* 29(3): 435–42. https://doi.org/10.1080/09512748.2016.1154678

Rendon, M. 2018. "When investment hurts: Chinese influence in Venezuela". Center for Strategic and International Studies. www.csis.org/analysis/when-investment-hurts-chinese-influence-venezuela

Ritchie, H. & M. Roser 2020. "CO_2 and greenhouse gas emissions". Our World in Data, May. https://ourworldindata.org/co2/country/china

RMF 2020. "Responsible Mining Index 2020". Responsible Mining Foundation. https://2020.responsibleminingindex.org/en/key-findings

Roberts, I. & A. Rush 2012. "Understanding China's demand for resource imports". *China Economic Review* 23(3): 566–79. https://doi.org/10.1016/j.chieco.2011.05.004

Rogelja, I. 2020. "Concrete and coal: China's infrastructural assemblages in the Balkans". *Political Geography* 81(Aug): 102220. https://doi.org/10.1016/j.polgeo.2020.102220

Rogelja, I. & K. Tsimonis 2020. "Narrating the China threat: securitising Chinese economic presence in Europe". *Chinese Journal of International Politics* 13(1): 103–33. https://doi.org/10.1093/cjip/poz019

Rolland, N. 2019a. *Securing the Belt and Road Initiative: China's Evolving Military Engagement along the Silk Roads*. Special Report no. 80. National Bureau of Asian Research. www.nbr.org/wp-content/uploads/pdfs/publications/sr80_securing_the_belt_and_road_sep2019.pdf

Rolland, N. 2019b. "A concise guide to the Belt and Road Initiative". National Bureau of Asian Research. www.nbr.org/publication/a-guide-to-the-belt-and-road-initiative/

Rotella, S. & K. Berg 2021. "Operation Fox Hunt: how China exports repression using a network of spies hidden in plain sight". *ProPublica*, 22 July. www.propublica.org/article/operation-fox-hunt-how-china-exports-repression-using-a-network-of-spies-hidden-in-plain-sight?token=SV45W9VHgigYbUE-m7o9xnvExqobnjcg

Roy, D. 1996. "The 'China Threat' issue: major arguments". *Asian Survey* 36(8): 758–71. https://doi.org/10.2307/2645437

Ryzhova, N. & G. Ioffe 2009. "Trans-border exchange between Russia and China: the case of Blagoveshchensk and Heihe". *Eurasian Geography and Economics* 50(3): 348–64. https://doi.org/10.2747/1539-7216.50.3.348

Sanderson, H. & M. Forsythe 2012. *China's Superbank: Debt, Oil and Influence: How China Development Bank Is Rewriting the Rules of Finance*. Chichester: Wiley.

SASAC 2018. "Economic performance of state-owned and state-holding enterprises from Jan to Apr in 2018". State-Owned Assets Supervision and Administration Commission of the State Council. 25 May. http://en.sasac.gov.cn/2018/05/25/c_4.htm

Schindler, S., J. DiCarlo & D. Paudel 2021. "The New Cold War and the rise of the 21st-century infrastructure state". *Transactions of the Institute of British Geographers* 47(2): 331–46. https://doi.org/10.1111/tran.12480

Schulhof, V., D. van Vuuren & J. Kirchherr 2022. "The Belt and Road Initiative (BRI): what will it look like in the future?" *Technological Forecasting and Social Change* 175(Feb). https://doi.org/10.1016/j.techfore.2021.121306

Segal, G. 1999. "Does China matter?" *Foreign Affairs*, October.

Segovia, M. 2021. "A dream deal with China that ended in nightmarish debt for Venezuela". *Dialogo Chino*, 14 February. https://dialogochino.net/en/trade-investment/40016-a-dream-deal-with-china-that-ended-in-nightmarish-debt-for-venezuela/

Seto, K. *et al.* 2016. "Carbon lock-in: types, causes, and policy implications". *Annual Review of Environment and Resources* 41(1): 425–52. https://doi.org/10.1146/annurev-environ-110615-085934

Sexton, J. 2011. *The Monroe Doctrine: Empire and Nation in Nineteenth-Century America.* New York, NY: Hill & Wang.

Sheives, K. 2006. "China turns west: Beijing's contemporary strategy towards Central Asia". *Pacific Affairs* 79(2): 205–24. https://doi.org/10.5509/2006792205

Shen, M. 2019. "'The Belt and Road', trade costs and new international development cooperation: the perspective of constructing regional economic development conditions ['一带一路', 贸易成本与新型国际发展合作—构建区域经济发展条件的视角]". *Journal of China Foreign Affairs University* [外交学院学报] 36(2): 1–28.

Shen, M. & Z. Zhang 2018. "Practical exploration and innovation of the Belt and Road financing mechanisms [一带一路'融资机制的实践探索与创新]". *Xin Shiye Expanding Horizons* 5: 27–34.

Shen, S. 2016. "How China's 'Belt and Road' compares to the Marshall Plan. Should we think of 'One Belt, One Road' as China's Marshall Plan?" *The Diplomat*, 6 February. https://thediplomat.com/2016/02/how-chinas-belt-and-road-compares-to-the-marshall-plan/

Shen, S. & W. Chan 2018. "A comparative study of the Belt and Road Initiative and the Marshall Plan". *Palgrave Communications* 4(1): 32. https://doi.org/10.1057/s41599-018-0077-9

Shesterinina, A. 2016. "Evolving norms of protection: China, Libya and the problem of intervention in armed conflict". *Cambridge Review of International Affairs* 29(3): 812–30. https://doi.org/10.1080/09557571.2016.1170103

Shvarts, E. & E. Fedichkina 2016. "Will Chinese factories pollute the Russian Far East?" WWF Amur Info Center. https://amurinfocenter.org/en/directions/green-economy/will-chinese-factories-pollute-the-russian-far-east/

Simangunsong, T. 2021. "Hydroelectric project in Sumatra risks extinction of World's rarest orangutan". *The Third Pole*, 3 September. www.thethirdpole.net/en/energy/potential-disaster-last-forest-sumatra/

Simon, F. 2021. "Official: western Balkan countries are 'milking coal power plants until the bitter end'". Euractiv.com. 10 June. www.euractiv.com/section/energy/interview/official-western-balkan-countries-are-milking-coal-power-plants-until-the-bitter-end/

Smil, V. 2013. *Making the Modern World: Materials and Dematerialization.* Chichester: Wiley.

Smith Finley, J. 2019. "Securitization, insecurity and conflict in contemporary Xinjiang: has PRC counter-terrorism evolved into state terror?" *Central Asian Survey* 38(1): 1–26. https://doi.org/10.1080/02634937.2019.1586348

Solomon, S. 2018. "Chinese officials arrested for bribery amid Kenya's SGR corruption inquiry". VOA, 26 November. www.voanews.com/a/china-kenya-bribery/4673798.html

Song, G. 2015. "The 'One Belt, One Road' strategic concept and the new development of China's economic diplomacy ['一带一路' 战略构想与中国经济外交新发展]". *International Observation* [国际观察] 4: 22–34.

Sorbello, P. 2021. "Kazakhstan's light rail corruption case drags on". *The Diplomat*, 16 October. https://thediplomat.com/2021/10/kazakhstans-light-rail-corruption-case-drags-on/

Steinberg, D. 2012. "On China–Myanmar relations". *Journal of Current Southeast Asian Affairs* 31(1): 3–6. https://doi.org/10.1177/186810341203100101

Stokke, O. (ed.) 2013. *Aid and Political Conditionality*. Abingdon: Routledge.

Stone, R. 2008. "The scope of IMF conditionality". *International Organization* 62(4): 589–620. https://doi.org/10.1017/S0020818308080211

Strachan, H. 2005. "The lost meaning of strategy". *Survival* 47(3): 33–54. https://doi.org/10.1080/00396330500248102

Strauss, J. 2009. "The past in the present: historical and rhetorical lineages in China's relations with Africa". *China Quarterly* 199(Sep): 777–95. https://doi.org/10.1017/S0305741009990208

Strauss, J. & A. Armony (eds) 2012. *From the Great Wall to the New World: China and Latin America in the 21st Century*. Cambridge: Cambridge University Press.

Summers, T. 2016. "China's 'New Silk Roads': sub-national regions and networks of global political economy". *Third World Quarterly* 37(9): 1628–43. https://doi.org/10.1080/01436597.2016.1153415

Summers, T. 2020. "Structural power and the financing of the Belt and Road Initiative". *Eurasian Geography and Economics* 61(2): 146–51. https://doi.org/10.1080/15387216.2020.1715234

Summers, T. 2021. "The Belt and Road Initiative in Southwest China: responses from Yunnan Province". *The Pacific Review* 34(2): 206–29. https://doi.org/10.1080/09512748.2019.1653956

Sun, I., K. Jayaram & O. Kassiri 2017. "Dance of the Lions and Dragons. How are Africa and China engaging, and how will the partnership evolve?" McKinsey & Co. www.mckinsey.com/~/media/mckinsey/featured%20insights/Middle%20East%20and%20Africa/The%20closest%20look%20yet%20at%20Chinese%20economic%20engagement%20in%20Africa/Dance-of-the-lions-and-dragons.ashx

Sun, L. 2022. "How can China's Belt and Road Initiative thrive when its members are at war?" *South China Morning Post*, 12 March. www.scmp.com/economy/china-economy/article/3170142/how-will-chinas-belt-and-road-initiative-fare-when-partners

Sun, Z. & N. Chen 2019. "An appraisement of the cooperation potential of cement production capacity of OBOR countries based on elasticity estimates: 2019–2028 [基于弹性估计的'一带一路'水泥产能合作潜力预测: 2019–2028]". *Journal of Xi'an University of Architecture and Technology (Social Science Edition)* [西安建筑科技大学学报(社会科学版)] 38(6): 48–57.

Tambo, E. *et al.* 2019. "China's Belt and Road Initiative: incorporating public health measures toward global economic growth and shared prosperity". *Global Health Journal* 3(2): 46–9. https://doi.org/10.1016/j.glohj.2019.06.003

Tani, S. 2019. "China-led AIIB to stay 'much leaner' than development bank peers". *Nikkei Asia*, 28 November. https://asia.nikkei.com/Editor-s-Picks/Interview/China-led-AIIB-to-stay-much-leaner-than-development-bank-peers

Tarnoff, C. 2018. "The Marshall Plan: design, accomplishments, and significance". *Congressional Research Service* 7–5700(Jan): 32.

Taylor, M. & S. Rioux 2018. *Global Labour Studies*. Cambridge: Polity.

Teo, H. *et al.* 2019. "Environmental impacts of infrastructure development under the Belt and Road Initiative". *Environments* 6(6): 72. https://doi.org/10.3390/environments6060072

Thar, C. & N. Aung 2020. "Kachin residents fearful of losing land to secretive China-backed industrial project". *Myanmar Now*, 7 July. www.myanmar-now.org/en/news/kachin-residents-fearful-of-losing-land-to-secretive-china-backed-industrial-project

Torres, A. *et al.* 2017. "A looming tragedy of the sand commons". *Science* 357(6355): 970–71. https://doi.org/10.1126/science.aao0503

Torres, A. *et al.* 2017. "The world is facing a global sand crisis". *The Conversation*, 7 September. http://theconversation.com/the-world-is-facing-a-global-sand-crisis-83557

Tower, J. & J. Staats 2020. "Is China getting serious about crime on the 'Belt and Road'?" USIP. 28 October. www.usip.org/publications/2020/10/china-getting-serious-about-crime-belt-and-road

Tracy, E. *et al.* 2017. "China's new Eurasian ambitions: the environmental risks of the Silk Road Economic Belt". *Eurasian Geography and Economics* 58(1): 56–88. https://doi.org/10.1080/15387216.2017.1295876

Transparency International 2011. Bribe Payers Index. https://issuu.com/transparencyinternational/docs/bribe_payers_index_2011?mode=window&backgroundColor=%23222222

Transparency International 2022. Corruption Perceptions Index – 2021. www.transparency.org/en/cpi/2021

Tsimonis, K. 2018. "Sharpening 'swords' and strengthening 'cages': anticorruption under Xi". In K. Brown (ed.), *China's 19th Party Congress: Start of a New Era*. 55–88, https://doi.org/10.1142/Q0177

Tsimonis, K. *et al.* 2019. "A synergy of failures: environmental protection and Chinese capital in southeast Europe". *Journal of Current Chinese Affairs* 48(2): 171–200. https://doi.org/10.1177/1868102620919861

Tsui, K.-y. & Y. Wang 2004. "Between separate stoves and a single menu: fiscal decentralization in China". *China Quarterly* 177(Mar): 71–90. https://doi.org/10.1017/S0305741004000050

Turcsányi, R. 2020. "China and the frustrated region: Central and Eastern Europe's repeating troubles with great powers". *China Report* 56(1): 60–77. https://doi.org/10.1177/0009445519895626

Uljevic, S. 2020. "The BRI is not at the end of the road". Eurasianet, 16 December. https://eurasianet.org/perspectives-the-bri-is-not-at-the-end-of-the-road

WALHI 2019. "Open letter to Bank of China". WALHI, 27 February. www.walhi.or.id/index.php/open-letter-to-bank-of-china

Wang, C. 2020. "China Belt and Road Initiative (BRI) Investment Report 2020". Green Finance Development Center. https://greenfdc.org/china-belt-and-road-initiative-bri-investment-report-2020/

Wang, C. 2021. "China Belt and Road Initiative (BRI) Investment Report 2021". Green Finance Development Center. https://greenfdc.org/brief-china-belt-and-road-initiative-bri-investment-report-2021/

Wang, P. & X. Yan 2020. "Bureaucratic slack in China: the anti-corruption campaign and the decline of patronage networks in developing local economies". *China Quarterly* 243(Sep): 611–34. https://doi.org/10.1017/S0305741019001504

Wang, Y., R. Morgan & M. Cashmore 2003. "Environmental impact assessment of projects in the People's Republic of China: new law, old problems". *Environmental Impact Assessment Review* 23(5): 543–79. https://doi.org/10.1016/S0195-9255(03)00071-4

Waruru, M. 2019. "Backers of Lamu coal project lose court case". *China Dialogue*, 4 July 2019. www.chinadialogue.net/article/show/single/en/11355-Backers-of-Lamu-coal-project-lose-court-case

Watts, J. 2010. *When a Billion Chinese Jump: How China Will Save Mankind – or Destroy It*. New York, NY: Scribner.

Weber, I. 2021. *How China Escaped Shock Therapy: The Market Reform Debate*. Abingdon: Routledge.

Wedeman, A. 2012. *Double Paradox: Rapid Growth and Rising Corruption in China*. Ithaca, NY: Cornell University Press.

Wilson, E. 2020. "China: end of the Belt and Road?" Euromoney, 4 June. www.euromoney.com/article/b1lx4xdjgghf3z/china-end-of-the-belt-and-road

Wong, A. 2018. "More than peripheral: how provinces influence China's foreign policy". *China Quarterly* 235(Sep): 735–57. https://doi.org/10.1017/S0305741018000930

Wong, E. 2013. "On scale of 0 to 500, Beijing's air quality tops 'crazy bad' at 755". *New York Times*, 13 January. www.nytimes.com/2013/01/13/science/earth/beijing-air-pollution-off-the-charts.html

World Bank 2020. World Governance Indicators – 2019. http://info.worldbank.org/governance/wgi/

Xi, J. 2013. "Promote friendship between our people and work together to build a bright future". FMPRC, 8 September. www.fmprc.gov.cn/ce/cebel/eng/zxxx/t1078088.htm

Xi, J. 2017. "Work together to build the Silk Road Economic Belt and the 21st Century Maritime Silk Road" [Speech by Xi Jinping]. Belt and Road Forum for International Cooperation, 14 May. http://2017.beltandroadforum.org/english/n100/2018/0306/c25-1038.html

Xi, J. 2019. "Working together to deliver a brighter future for the Belt and Road Cooperation". The Second Belt and Road Forum for International Cooperation, 26 April. www.beltandroadforum.org/english/n100/2019/0426/c22-1266.html

Xi, J. 2022. "Keynote Speech at the Opening Ceremony of the Boao Forum for Asia Annual Conference 2022". Ministry of Foreign Affairs of the People's Republic of China. 21 April. www.fmprc.gov.cn/mfa_eng/zxxx_662805/202204/t20220421_10671083.html

Xinhua 2017. "Xi Jinping meets with the 2017 work conference of diplomatic envoys abroad and delivers an important speech [习近平接见2017年度驻外使节工作会议与会使节并发表重要讲话-新华网]". Xinhuanet.com, 28 December. www.xinhuanet.com/politics/leaders/2017-12/28/c_1122181743.htm

Xue, L. 2015. "Diplomatic risks facing China's Belt and Road Initiative ['一带一路' 战略面对的外交风险]". *International Economic Review* [国际经济评论] 2: 68–79.

Yan, H. & B. Sautman 2013. "'The beginning of a world empire'? Contesting the discourse of Chinese copper mining in Zambia". *Modern China* 39(2): 131–64. https://doi.org/10.1177/0097700412473705

Yan, X. 1995. "China's post-Cold War security strategy". *Contemporary International Relations* 5(5).

Yang, Z. 2021. "Ministry says fugitive's repatriation shows determination to fight corruption". *China Daily*, 16 November 2021. www.global.chinadaily.com.cn/a/202111/16/WS6192f0d3a310cdd39bc757b9.html

Ye, M. 2020. *The Belt Road and Beyond: State-Mobilized Globalization in China: 1998–2018*. Cambridge: Cambridge University Press.

Ye, M. 2021. "Fragmented motives and policies: the Belt and Road Initiative in China". *Journal of East Asian Studies* 21(2): 193–217. https://doi.org/10.1017/jea.2021.15

Yoeli, M. 2021. "Belt and Road in Kenya: Covid-19 sparks a reckoning with debt and dissatisfaction". Council of Foreign Relations. www.cfr.org/blog/belt-and-road-kenya-covid-19-sparks-reckoning-debt-and-dissatisfaction

Zeng, J. 2019. "Narrating China's belt and road initiative". *Global Policy* 10(2): 207–16.

Zenz, A. & J. Leibold 2017. "Chen Quanguo: the strongman behind Beijing's securitization strategy in Tibet and Xinjiang". *China Brief* 17(12). https://jamestown.org/program/chen-quanguo-the-strongman-behind-beijings-securitization-strategy-in-tibet-and-xinjiang/

Zhai, K. 2015. "Strategic thinking on the construction of 'One Belt One Road' ['一带一路' 建设的战略思考]". *International Observation* [国际观察] 4: 49–60.

Zhang, A. 2014. "Bureaucratic politics and China's anti-monopoly law". *Cornell International Law Journal* 47(3): 671–708.

Zhang, C. 2016. "Has China's impact assessment law lost its teeth?" *China Dialogue*, 20 July. https://chinadialogue.net/en/pollution/9122-has-china-s-impact-assessment-law-lost-its-teeth/

Zhang, C. 2019. "How much do state-owned enterprises contribute to China's GDP and employment?" Working Paper 140361. The World Bank. https://documents.worldbank.org/en/publication/documents-reports/documentdetail/449701565248091726/How-Much-Do-State-Owned-Enterprises-Contribute-to-China-s-GDP-and-Employment

Zhang, H. 2020. "The aid-contracting nexus: the role of the international contracting industry in China's overseas development engagements". *China Perspectives* 2020(4): 17–27. https://doi.org/10.4000/chinaperspectives.11124

Zhang, Y. & S. Chen 2021. "Wood trade responses to ecological rehabilitation program: evidence from China's new logging ban in natural forests". *Forest Policy and Economics* 122(Jan): 102339. https://doi.org/10.1016/j.forpol.2020.102339

Zhao, K. 2016. "Research on China's strategy of 'One Belt One Road' ['一带一路' 的中国方略研究]". *Journal of Xinjiang Normal University* [新疆师范大学学报] 37(1): 22–33.

Zhao, M. 2018. "The major power competition and the US counterbalance against the Belt and Road Initiative [大国竞争背景下美国对 '一带一路' 的制衡态势论析]". *World Economy and Politics* [世界经济与政治] 12: 4–31.

Zhou, F. 2015. "Risks and challenges facing the Belt and Road Initiative and their countermeasures ['一带一路'面临的风险挑战及其应对]". *Guoji Guancha*.

Zhu, K., R. Shi & R. Lempert 2021. "Recalibrating the Belt and Road Initiative amidst deep uncertainties". *Journal of Mega Infrastructure & Sustainable Development*, December. https://doi.org/10.1080/24724718.2021.1983281

Zolinger Fujii, W. 2021. "'My order, my rules': China and the American rules-based order in historical perspective". *E-International Relations*, December. www.e-ir.info/2021/12/28/my-order-my-rules-china-and-the-american-rules-based-order-in-historical-perspective/

Zou, M. 2019. "China and the Belt and Road Initiative: transnational labor law under state capitalism 4.0". *AJIL Unbound* 113: 418–23. https://doi.org/10.1017/aju.2019.76

Zoubir, Y. & E. Tran 2021. "China's health Silk Road in the Middle East and North Africa amidst COVID-19 and a contested world order". *Journal of Contemporary China*, August, 1–16. https://doi.org/10.1080/10670564.2021.1966894

Index